C0-DKM-949

Latin American

Woman:

The meek speak out

Edited by June H. Turner

Photographs by Joseph W. Conyard

Published by International Educational
Development, Inc.

108643

LATIN AMERICAN WOMAN: THE MEEK SPEAK OUT. Copyright © 1980 by International Educational Development, Inc. and June Haney Turner. All rights reserved in the United States of America. No part of this book may be used or reproduced in any manner whatsoever without written permission except in the case of brief quotations embodied in critical articles and reviews. For information address International Educational Development/June H. Turner, P.O. Box 66, Silver Spring, Maryland 10907.

FIRST EDITION

Library of Congress Catalog Card No.: 81-80844

Turner, June H., ed.
  Latin American Woman.

Silver Spring, Md. : International
Educational Development, Inc.

230 p.

8104   810226
ISBN No. 0-939420-00-7

THE MEEK SPEAK OUT

CONTENTS

INTRODUCTION

In Latin America, women generally play supportive rather than leading roles in society. The region's institutions, such as the Church, political bodies, government bureaucracies, education, and the family, are all predicated on women's support but do not tend to place woman in the "Number One" position, regardless of her education and social level. If she finds herself in this situation, it is usually by default rather than design.

It is generally recognized that women represent a potentially formidable force for accelerating economic and social development, particularly at the lowest income level and in rural communities. There are increasing numbers of professionally trained, capable women who are committing their efforts to helping their disadvantaged "sisters" to improve their lives and the poor communities in which they live and raise their families. Many are, themselves, from poor communities, but have managed to pull themselves up by their "sandal-straps," and are currently carrying out programs designed to overcome the barriers poverty places in the road to development and social change. The tendency, however, is to use them as workers and ignore or overlook their opinions and counsel. Few hold decision- or policy-making positions, and even fewer are heads of organizations.

There are, of course, notable exceptions. It is also true that women in leadership positions are a minority everywhere in the world, not in Latin America alone. *Latin American Woman: The Meek Speak Out* is not intended to imply that it represents all women, or even all Latin American women. Rather, it is the result of International Educational Development's (IED) concern for the felt needs and problems of women that have come to our attention during the course of our Network Program.

Public support for projects to develop women's expertise is essential to maximizing their effectiveness. Such projects are most successful when implemented by competent and capable women who have the confidence and trust of those they are trying to assist. Yet the image of this woman who has involved herself by choice in grassroots development is vague to the outside world, and public knowledge of her work is fragmented. There is no role model. And because funding organizations have greater access to and knowledge about programs headed by men who assure them that women are an integral part of their planning, they tend to devote minimal support to areas where assistance is needed most.

Development planners and funding agencies often base decision-making about women's projects on insufficient or superficial information. Until adequate information about poor rural women's needs and the many efforts of capable women to respond to them is more adequately defined and made accessible, policymakers will continue to make development decisions in a vacuum, and available financial and technical resources will make limited impact on social change.

The women whose points of view are included in this anthology come from eight countries: Bolivia, Peru, Colombia and Ecuador, in South America; and from Costa Rica, Nicaragua, Honduras and El Salvador, in Central America. They do not pretend to be professional writers. They have committed their lives and work to help poor women help themselves. Representing a wide variety of experience, educational backgrounds and national idiosyncrasies, they range from a rural nurse's aide to a Doctor of Philosophy in Education, from a Catholic nun to a former political activist turned bank executive.

Two of the group are not native Latin Americans. Anita Carlier, Dutch by birth, was included because of her unique experience and commitment to poor rural women in the Peruvian Andes. Bambi Arellano is a second generation Argentinian on her mother's side, but was born in the United States. Her analysis of the Bolivian perspective is unusually objective. Both Carlier and Arellano bring to the book a degree of critical frankness that speaks for itself.

IED's objective in compiling this anthology was to call to the attention of educators, policy-makers, project planners, implementors and funding agencies the kinds of projects that are contributing to a new status for women. We believe that those whose articles are included have something to say that is worth listening to, that their experiences and ideas as expressed in relation to their own environment should be heard by persons whose responsibilities and interests lie in Latin American development in particular, and Third World women in general.

We began in early 1979 by inviting this group of thirteen to write about their personal experiences and work with women in their respective countries. They were especially selected because of their professional expertise, their commitment to their work, and their credibility with and acceptance by the women they work with. Their articles deal openly with the effects of attitudes, prejudices, value systems, and stereotypes held by society toward poor women. They discuss the problems of rebuilding the self-confidence of these women on whom centuries of oppression has left a heavy weight of suspicion and distrust. IED believes that these monographs cast new light on what is needed to work successfully with poor rural women and that nebulous sector of the population casually referred to by international development agencies as "the poorest of the poor."

The book attempts to present the authors in as personal a way as possible so that the reader might become acquainted with "who" each woman is and why. For this reason, Joe Conyard, President of IED, photographed each in her own country and when possible, in her work environment as well. Because of the political unrest in El Salvador and Nicaragua at the time the book was being compiled, we were unable to include photographs of the two authors from those countries. The anthology, however, has no intended political message. The broad spectrum of contemporary viewpoints provides a meaningful overview for those who wish to familiarize themselves with the diversity of feminine thought in Latin America which is as different as the countries themselves.

IED gratefully acknowledges all the assistance that has made the publication of this book possible. We particularly wish to thank the Consortium for Community Self-Help and its director, Blanche Case, as well as Howard Landis of Oxford Lithograph, and Private Agencies Collaborating Together (P.A.C.T.) for their financial assistance. We are indebted to Paula Diebold de Cruz, Norma Romano de Benner, Caridad Inda and Mark R. Turner for their valuable assistance in translating the articles from the original Spanish in which they were written and for their editorial advice. We are especially grateful to Nicholas Satieha/Stock, Boston, Inc. for the cover photograph, to Dr. Sam Apeji, Faculty of Agriculture, Ahmadu Bello University, Zaria, Nigeria, for his photograph of the editor, and to Jaqueline Berthet for the cover design of the book and her art work which she contributed because she believed in the project. Very special thanks is also due to Mercedes Sanguinetty who not only helped with the translating, but also worked for many hours typing the original manuscript. And lastly, we are indebted to the women who wrote the articles for the book, for without their willingness to speak out, the message would not be heard.

June Haney Turner, General Editor
December 1980

SQUATTER SETTLEMENT

DECISION-MAKING:

FOR MEN ONLY?

Carmen Arimana Alva (Peru)

Carmen Arimana Alva is a gentle woman. She is warm, motherly, and one immediately feels at home in her presence. There is a sense that this warmth has come from experience, strength and suffering borne of love. She reflects pride in her Peruvian heritage, in her Quechua surname—" 'Ari' means 'yes' while 'mana' says 'no' "—and in her parents, both of whom were born in Ica. She smiles as she says of her father, "He was a 'serrano-morachuco,'[1] you know; the family was from Ayacucho."

Carmen, however, grew up in Lima. Her great desire was to become a doctor although this was not considered the proper profession for young ladies. After her graduation from secondary studies at the School of the Sacred Heart[2] in 1947, still with medicine in mind, she postponed entering the university because of her mother's health.

In 1949, Carmen entered the University of San Marcos' San Fernando School of Medicine. After four years at San Marcos, she was obliged to discontinue her studies again for financial reasons, and went to work for a private organization where she became engrossed in the labor movement, an interest which has been indirectly responsible for leading her from medicine to social work with the "pueblos jovenes."

She was awarded three separate "scholarships" by labor groups, intended to encourage her continued interest in their organizations.[3] The last of these took her to the United States for three months, but upon return to Peru, Carmen found her job had been abolished along with others at the private organization. She was immediately offered a contract by the Peruvian Center for Labor Studies to supervise their national education and training program, taking her from one end of the country to the other.

During this time, one of her students, Fr. Joseph Kearny, was a Roman Catholic priest. He and Carmen began discussing the problems of the workers in the "pueblos jovenes," and concluded that the labor unions helped the people who had

---

[1] Legend has it that the "morachucos," fair-skinned and often with European features, were descended from the ex-communicated Spaniards who rebelled against Pizarro and took refuge among the horsemen of the Quechua tribes that dominated the Andean highland plains at the time of the Spanish conquest.

[2] Colegio Religiosas Reparadoras del Sagrado Corazon, a primary and secondary school for girls, located in the Lima suburb of Lince.

[3] The International Federation of Employees and Technicians; the Peruvian Center for Labor Studies; and the American Institute for Free Labor Development (Washington, D.C.).

jobs, but only at their places of employment. They asked themselves, "Who is assisting the ones who don't have jobs? Who is doing anything in the squatter settlements where the workers and their families live?" They conceded that the latter problem represented the vast majority who migrated to Lima, and spent many hours discussing what to do about it. And so, the Association Team for Human Development (EDH)[4] was conceived.

Carmen has suffered many frustrations, not the least of which was a result of some of her own experiences with the labor organizations for which she worked. She feels herself a part of the world of workers, but not a part of the partisan political movements that use the workers to compete for power. She was "practically expelled" as a result of her beliefs, and is proud to say that the EDH has neither political nor religious ties or biases. "This sometimes presents a problem," she will tell you, "because astute individuals who can see EDH's potential from a self-serving point of view, are always offering to help. It is always difficult to turn money away, especially when it is the thing you need the most."

Carmen's greatest hope is that the EDH will be able to find a more permanent source of funding for their work. The organization has only six full-time paid personnel and finding the financial support to pay their salaries and carry on the work without succumbing to partisan interest is a continual thorn. The fact that the majority of the staff is volunteer, makes it even more imperative that those who direct the organization be free to devote their full time to planning, providing continuity and leadership. Without a more dependable source of income, Carmen never knows for certain from one month to the next, whether they will be able to meet the creditors.

Carmen, separated from her husband, lives alone with her son, a university student.

---

[4]Asociacion *Equipo para el Desarrollo Humano* (Spanish name), a private, non-profit voluntary organization, legally registered with the Government of Peru. The organization is dedicated to social and economic development, and opportunities for the poor.

SQUATTER SETTLEMENT DECISION-MAKING: FOR MEN ONLY?

by

Carmen Arimana Alva

Editor's note: *A phenomena of Lima in the early 60's were the "invasores," as they were called in those days: "invaders," or rural migrants who moved to the city overnight, en masse, with their blankets and babies on their backs. As many as 10,000 to 25,000 at a time would illegally settle themselves on unused government lands around the fringe of the city. They would hoist the national flag; put down their cane stakes; throw up walls of cardboard or grass matting; unroll their blankets; and call it "mi casa." There were no utilities—no water, no sanitation, no electricity, no nothing—only sandy dirt and dust. These people, composed mostly of young parents with children, were crowded together in the most frightful promiscuity, yet conditions in the sierra were sufficiently bad and the job expectancy in Lima sufficiently alluring, that these "squatter settlements" not only survived, but grew.*

Once a colony was established, relatives or friends from the countryside moved in with the family or built new shacks, sometimes doubling up on a small parcel of land. The great majority sought employment in the city.

The first task, however, was organizing defense against forcible removal by the police or military. Thus began the first community associations which later played a key role in organizing cooperative efforts to improve the squatter settlements. Some represented only a half-dozen members who met occasionally to share their miseries. Others grew to complex structures that some 20 years later, now involve blocks, sections and central committees; regulate the community in detail and press actively for major improvements.

Some are firmly non-partisan; others have become virtually part of the formal organization of the dominant local political party, and operate as local party machines.

In some of the older settlements, stories of voluntary groups laying pipelines, constructing a school, church or community center are history. So, too, are the tales of the efforts that failed or were aborted. Most major improvements require at least some assistance from local authorities; therefore, the response of the government is as important as the efforts of the settlers. This is usually pursued by petitioning the support of a prominent politician or public figure and, while not always successful, has been the means by which at least two of the larger and older settlements, have been converted into municipalities of greater Lima. In the summer of 1968, thousands of "barriada"[1] residents gathered and carefully rehearsed a march on the Presidential Palace to demand that they be granted title to their land. A strong and widely known leader organized the demonstration. As the settlements have been legitimized, at least politically, they have acquired the more socially acceptable name of "pueblos jovenes," or "new towns."

---

[1] Peruvians use the term *"barriada"* to refer to low income neighborhoods and slum areas.

Collectively, they house about a third to half of Lima's urban population. In addition to large numbers of service workers and smaller numbers of artisans and factory workers, the settlements often include a sprinkling of white-collar clerks, shop assistants, teachers, low-level functionaries such as police and firemen, and occasional professionals.

As the settlement becomes better established and its needs are gradually met, residents' consensus and priorities shift to other issues which must be pursued individually or through organizations based on ties other than residence—such as unions and professional associations. However, in the beginning, inhabitants of the newer and smaller settlements are largely on their own.

Carmen Arimana Alva's article revolves around two related "pueblos jovenes," "Pamplona I" and "Pamplona Alta." "Pamplona I" is one of the older larger settlements which now has a population of about 150,000. Most of its streets are paved and it now has electricity, piped water and schools. It is filled with success stories. "Pamplona II" takes up where "Pamplona I" leaves off; that is, where the pavement and the electricity and the water stop.

The sun, filtered bleakly through the fog low on the horizon and the sounds of families —babies crying, a radio playing rock music, a dog barking, a mother shouting at her children and, very softly, the sad notes of a *"pinkull'u"*[2]—provided a backdrop for the patched-up shacks marching up and down the dry brown hills. The sky seemed an enormous gray expanse. There were no trees to soften its austerity, no grass or flowers to add a note of gaiety or color. Ragged, barefooted children followed at my heels as I trudged up the dusty street. When I came to the gray adobe wall behind which were two of our now abandoned classrooms, I rattled the wooden gate, calling loudly to Victoria at the same time, "Victoria, open up! Open up!"

Within seconds, Victoria lifted the heavy wooden bar that latched the gate, and shyly greeted me, "Come in, Senora—you surprised me. I didn't think to see anyone this time of day."

Although it was approaching the time for preparing the evening meal, there was no smell of food cooking. I followed her into the yard which was flanked on one side by the abandoned classrooms, and by her small hut on the other. It was such a pity, I thought, that the community did not continue the classes here. Now the two latrines are being wasted, not to mention the cooking equipment that's going to rot and ruin. All because a couple of poor souls broke in one night and made off with some of the things. Even though the thieves had returned what they had stolen when they heard the classrooms were being shut down, the group felt they could not risk investing more equipment in a place that was so easy to break into. They had offered Victoria, a *"campesina"* from the sierra, a place for her and her

---

[2]A *"pinkull'u"* is a small flute-like musical instrument made and played by the Andean mountain folk of Peru. It is a simple narrow wooden tube about six inches long. There are four holes on the top side which, in effect, produce the different notes when the fingers are placed over them or released at the same time as air is blown through the tube. The instrument produces sad, haunting high-pitched music, usually played in a minor key.

baby to live, in return for watching the property, poor as it was.

A small brown mongrel, the color of the sandy dirt, growled peevishly at me with his tail between his legs, as Victoria invited me into the house to see the baby. I stepped over three or four bedraggled chickens that huddled against the doorstep, too small to either eat or to lay eggs. Inside the house, the little room was as "neat as a pin." There was a small wooden table covered with a worn, but clean piece of "oil cloth" and two crude wooden chairs. There were two fresh wildflowers in a bottle on the table and a candle ready to be lighted which, aside from one small window, was the only source of illumination. Next to the wall was a small, home-made crib in which the child lay.

Victoria picked up the child and held it close. Although I knew it to be almost two years old, it couldn't have weighed over seven pounds. The tiny thing was listless, unresponsive and its little eyes, dull and unfocused. Its head wobbled pathetically. "He is not well," she told me, "I know he is hungry, but I have nothing to feed him."

"I thought you were nursing him. Don't you have any milk?" I asked.

"I nursed him for awhile, but they told me I should stop—that bending over all the time with my breasts full of milk wasn't good for me," she told me, "so I let my milk dry up."

16

"Who told you that?" I questioned.

"The doctor at the clinic," she replied. "He said it was better to feed the baby formula."

The child appeared to be on the verge of starvation and was probably permanently retarded, mentally. "And are you feeding him on formula?" I persisted.

"Oh, no—not now. I tried, but the *'bodega'*[3] doesn't have it anymore. I was only able to buy one can," she said, "but before I used it all, I ran out of water. See..." she said, hopefully, "I still have some left." She held up a small can of powdered milk formula. The entire can would perhaps have provided enough for two or three days at most. "I tried to buy more, but I don't even have enough money for water, so it's useless."

"What do you mean, you 'ran out of water?' Hasn't the truck been by?"

Victoria lives in the more recently settled part of Pamplona Alta, in a *"barriada"* that has no water piped in. The residents in this area generally build cement brick cisterns or holding tanks on top of the ground in front of the house. Tank trucks filled with water, service the area once or twice a week, charging about U.S. $2.00 to fill up the tank.

"Oh, it comes by, but it won't stop. I haven't had fresh water, except what I can borrow from the neighbors, for several weeks."

"I don't understand. Why won't it stop?"

"Because," she replied, averting my eyes, "they know I don't have any money to pay for it. One time they filled up the tank before I told them I couldn't pay right away—now, they won't stop anymore."

The majority of those who live in the *"pueblos jovenes"* have migrated to the city from rural areas, particularly from the Andean sierra. Dreaming of a better future for their children, they are attracted to Lima by the "bright lights," and all the grand things they have heard about the Capital. Because there is no work in their rural communities, the unknown offers hope—hope of employment, hope for education, hope for better living conditions. Like migrating birds, the flight to the city is almost instinctive, but contrary to expectations, results in having to survive great hardships. Where they have had open skies and freedom of the fields, they now find themselves constrained by rules, regulations, laws, and procedures which seem designed to prevent them from achieving their hopes. Since a large percentage, especially the women, are illiterate, the signs, directions, and newspapers that could be helpful, are meaningless. They find themselves unable to communicate in their own land, unable to find jobs, and confused by urban customs and systems never encountered previously. Lacking any specific training or education, it requires almost superhuman determination and perseverance to move, economically and socially, beyond the poverty of the *"barriadas"* which often are cruel human jungles in themselves. At this point, the dream becomes a nightmare.

---

[3]Peruvians use the Spanish word *"bodega"* to indicate the "corner grocery store."

We at EDH consider it necessary that the first step in working with the people of the *"pueblos jovenes"* is to help them discover their true worth as persons. They must believe they are worthy of respect and deserve opportunities for self-realization as human beings. Such opportunities can only be acquired through education in its various forms, through the experience of work and participation, through decision-making and carrying out plans to develop the community as a whole, and through sharing in the life and future of the country as responsible citizens.

Our work at the *Asociacion Equipo Para el Desarrollo Humano* (EDH) (Human Development Team) is committed to providing the inhabitants of the *"pueblos jovenes"* with the opportunity to acquire training and access to knowledge and information that will help them to improve their lives as individuals and as communities. Necessarily, this involves all persons, both men and women, but it is extremely difficult to integrate women into this educational process. Women, all too often, consider that they are only good for raising children and attending to the needs of men, nothing else. Women are victims of double discrimination—by family because they are women, and by society because they are illiterate, poor women—and what is worse, they don't even know it.

This obvious problem which we faced each day in our work with the *"pueblos jovenes,"* led EDH to develop and initiate a program addressed exclusively to women. This program has been in process since 1975, in eighteen sectors of *Pamplona Alta,*[4] a settlement with over 150,000 inhabitants, as well as others[5] in the area south of Lima known as the "southern cone."

Our Program for the Promotion of Women was based on a variety of "clubs" and "women's associations" that already existed in the *"barriadas."* All of these groups had been formed for the purpose of providing help to "outstanding mothers," such as gifts on Mother's Day and Christmas. The recipients were always those who had been victimized: the burdened mother with the most children, the abandoned mother, the one having the most difficult time. Raised to be meek and submissive, and believing that to suffer is the natural role of woman, these groups rewarded those who had sacrificed and suffered most, making the martyr the model. This has the effect of making the victim a symbol of success for all mothers.

EDH sees a different future for the women of the *"pueblos jovenes"* which can only be accomplished by liberating women from their traditional attitudes and resignation to the role of suffering and submission. We believe, instead, that a woman should enjoy being a woman, and that this enjoyment comes from knowing your own worth as a human being. EDH's objective is to mobilize the potential and make it a reality.

The government's National Support System for Social Mobilization (SINAMOS)[6] stated it was the duty of community organizations in the *"pueblos jovenes"* to be models of social democracy with full participation of the people. It decreed that such participation be achieved through the election of representatives from each block or neighborhood committee consisting of twenty to thirty families. These representatives became the Promotion and Development Committee of the *"pueblo,"* over which presided a Central Governing Board elected from among its members. Obviously, no document mentioned it and no one suggested it, but initially all persons elected as leaders of the community organizations were men.

Women were simply not taken into account. Neither did any mention the possibility or desire to be elected; they had their "Mother's Club" or "Center"—period.

One of the first things we did was to contact all of the neighborhood representatives to the *"pueblo's"* Promotion and Development Committee, both individually and in groups. The purpose was to help them "discover" together that, without sharing of responsibility by the *"pueblo"* women, it would be impossible to meet the demands of SINAMOS for full community participation. It was imperative that the male leaders recognize the importance of integrating women into the Communities.

Simultaneously, we held meetings with the women's groups to help them analyze and question the "insatiable" objective of their activities, and to motivate them to

---

[4]These eighteen sectors include San Francisco de la Cruz, Nuevo Horizonte, 28 de Mayo, Buenos Milagros, Los Angeles, Los Laureles, Virgin del Buen Paso, Leonidas Prado, 1° de Mayo, Ampliacion, Brillante, 12 de Noviembre, 5 de Mayo, Miguel Grau, Ollanta, 3 de Julio.

[5]The settlements in the municipality of Chorrillos including Santa Teresa and Miguel Iglesias; and seven in the municipality of Surcos: Cocharcas, Buenos Aires, Vista Alegre, 3 de Octubre, San Juan de la Libertad, Sta. Teresa de Villa, and Delicias de Villa.

[6]The *"Sistema Nacional de Apoyo a la Movilizacion Social,"* created by the Revolutionary Government of the Armed Forces, is no longer active.

express their opinions on why women were not involved in the community organization. "How," we asked, "can you accept the fact that the assemblies are for men only and you can't attend when *you* are the ones who spend the greater part of your lives in the community itself—not in Lima or traveling back and forth—*you*, who struggle with the rats, sick children, washing the clothes when there is no water and lack of health services and sanitation all day long, as well as at night...?"

Of course, our objective at that time was not to persuade them to attend or participate in the community organization meetings, or to get themselves elected as representatives to the organization. In truth, they were not ready for this. Rather, our plan was to try to transform the existing "mother's clubs" and "centers" into centers for the "promotion of women," and where no women's organizations existed, to create them. Our goal was to encourage, develop and support the conscious, positive and coordinated participation of women in the programs and activities of the community organization. By integrating the women and men, we hoped to improve and strengthen community action. At no time was our purpose to place women in confrontation or competition with the men, but rather:

—To provide to women in the *"pueblos jovenes,"* the guidance they requested to help them broaden their understanding of their role within the family, as well as to the home as a base, but not their *only* sphere of interest and action;

—To increase the establishment of stronger and more positive family ties that will lead to greater cooperation among its members, and acceptance by them of the new, dynamic role women can play if they choose to develop themselves as persons;

—To promote the idea and support the creation of a neighborhood organization to represent and channel the efforts of each woman to improve herself, until such time as it is possible to integrate its members into the larger Community Organization;

—To offer training and guidance to women leaders, both active and potential, supporting and channeling their initiatives and projects.

EDH decided that it would make the goal and objectives of its Program for the Promotion of Women known to women's groups in the *"pueblos jovenes,"* but would direct the program only to those who request it.

Other characteristics of the Program are:

—Participation will never be denied on the basis of legal status, political or religious beliefs, income level, or level of instruction or education attained;

—It is intended for women seventeen years of age and older;

—Attendance and participation is voluntary, but responsible; there is no pressure exerted on members to attend, nor "rewards" offered for any purpose. No registration is required; the mere fact of living in the neighborhood is considered sufficient basis for participation;

—There are no dues or financial obligations to "keep the organization solvent;"

—The program functions as an open group at the neighborhood level, with elected leaders, and is completely autonomous in its decision-making, although directly linked to and coordinated with the [male-dominated] Neighborhood Committee.

The relationship between each neighborhood "Center for the Promotion of Women" and EDH, is based on faith in the potential and emerging capability of the women's groups to assume responsibility and make decisions, and deep respect for the dignity of woman as a human being.

While we achieved a high level of motivation and participation among the *"barriada"* women in those early years, it was obvious that the neighborhood "Centers for the Promotion of Women" were not receiving the formal support of the local [all male] "Neighborhood Committees." The *"barriada"* representatives were skeptical, and within the family, the men (fathers, husbands, brothers and sons) viewed the groups with anything but enthusiasm. Their reactions ranged from ridicule to rejection, complaining that "meetings two or three times a week only serve to waste time" that the woman "ought to be" spending at home. I remember one who sneered, "I'm all for 'the development of women,' *senora,*[7] but I haven't seen any signs of physical improvement yet."

At fault, in part, is the great national unemployment problem, together with the fact that women are not trained to do anything that takes them out of the home part or all of the day.

A great percentage are illiterate. Actually, the man does not oppose his wife working; on the contrary, he rather finds it quite to his advantage. He does oppose the woman wanting to prepare herself from the "human development" standpoint because he doesn't understand what this means and cannot see how it will benefit him. Most of the men believed the women were "getting together" to gossip.

This opinion gradually began to change, and continues changing ever so slowly — but positively. The women met, and still meet for work sessions involving information, guidance, and discussions on family life and education. Specific courses have been requested by the participants such as: pattern design and cutting, first aid, nutrition, raising and educating the child, family relationships, family budget, handicrafts and various manual skills. The course on family education served to make the men more aware that they could, indeed, benefit from better management of the home, as well as some of the advantages to be gained by awakening the woman to her new role as a companion in place of the traditional house servant. The majority of the men we have talked to indicate they are very pleased with the improvements they see taking place in their women, both in their behavior and their skills.

Marta, a *"senora"* in the *"barriada"* San Francisco de la Cruz, is a good example of what can be accomplished by promoting women. She has eleven children and a permanent smile from ear to ear that describes her happiness better than anything else. She has a well-ordered home, has been president of the Parents' Association where her children attend school. First, Marta used the cooking skills she learned from the EDH course to work in a restaurant; then, she decided she would learn

---

[7] A married woman.

some wood-working skills so she could help her husband who is a carpenter. A little later, she took our course in knitting and now, in addition to her other skills, she is selling purses, shawls, and other hand-knitted items in downtown Lima. She was also president of the *"barriada"* Center for the Promotion of Women. Many husbands like Marta's who used to oppose their attending courses and discussions involved in "promoting women," now are very proud of their wives. It is becoming quite common for the elected male representatives to the community organizations to send their wives in their place when they are unable to attend the meetings.

We began to notice a great change in the attitudes of the men around 1974, when our program in Pamplona Alta began emphasizing civic education and community participation for women. At this point, the Community Organization, for the first time, began to incorporate women into its leadership. The Center for the Promotion of Women's representative was given a seat on the Central Board of Directors. Currently, there is no *"barriada"* in Pamplona Alta that does not have women representatives filling positions of leadership on the individual neighborhood committees, the Promotion and Development Committee or the Central Board of Directors.

Now that the women are being integrated into the daily work plans of the Community Organization, EDH has begun to lower the profile of its efforts with the Centers for the Promotion of Women in many *"barriadas."* It is no longer necessary to expend the energy of our small staff in the neighborhoods where we have accomplished most of what we set out to do. The women are demonstrating the benefits of our guidance and training, of having learned to work together, and are now quite capable of carrying on with only nominal assistance from EDH.

We began working in Pamplona in 1970, when there was no water, no electricity, and nothing you could call streets. There was absolutely nothing but dirt and 60,000 people. Today, there are over 150,000 and over half have electricity. Almost everyone is from the "sierra" and as the flow of new arrivals continues, Pamplona is expanding outward and upward into dusty, semi-rural hills on its outer edge. Usually the first members of the family to migrate are the ones who

22

can get employment—then, as they spot a little piece of unused land "up the hill," grandmother and uncle arrive. We have come a long way in a few short years, but at the rate the people continue arriving from the sierra, we have a long way to go before we run out of work.

The groups of women we work with include a large percentage of unwed mothers and abandoned women. They are the most difficult. They are not usually members of a *"barriada"* family and thus, have no security, cannot rely on extended family to care for the child, and have nowhere to turn for help. Although initial groups that organize as "squatters" usually screen out unattached, single adults, as the settlements age they become more heterogenous. Community associations continue to try, with varying success, to screen out so-called "undesirables." Life is perhaps hardest of all for women like Victoria, who I mentioned earlier, that fall into this category. Unfortunately, they are numerous. Those who participate in the EDH Program encounter support and possibilities for changing their situations, but it is one of the most difficult areas within which to achieve success without the help of government and the understanding of society.

Nevertheless, the success of the Program for the Promotion of Women is underscored by two additional undertakings which have grown out of it. The first, our Child Development Program, came about in order to help mothers who wanted to, but could not regularly attend our courses and discussions at the neighborhood centers. Many had referred to the problem of not having anyone to look after their pre-school children which resulted either in irregular attendance, or having to bring the children with them. In the latter case, we found when the little ones made a fuss, the mothers could not pay attention, and consequently, it was impossible to carry on a normal meeting. Thus emerged the day-care centers.

These centers for the children functioned initially in temporary locations and people's homes. Now the program is housed in buildings constructed specifically for this purpose, and it operates with the approval of and in coordination with the Ministry of Education's official Non-formal Basic Education Program. Centers are located in Pamplona Alta and in the *"pueblos jovenes"* of Chorrillos and Sucre. Each has its "parent's committee" comprising mothers and fathers who see that all the parents participate in the running of the center, and the coordination of its activities with the Community Organization.

Local *"barriada"* women are nominated by the "parent's committees" as candidates to fill the need for volunteer "teachers" at the day-care centers. The proposed candidates are screened for certain characteristics that ensure they can become good instructors, and those selected are trained by the EDH team, with the help of the Ministry of Education. This procedure guarantees the level of pre-school preparation provided to the children who attend.

The second effort that has stemmed from the "Promotion of Women" is our Community Health Field-Worker Training Program. The Program is designed to train local neighborhood women as volunteer community health workers because of the overwhelming need of the poor in the *"pueblos jovenes"* for medical attention. These large and expanding populations cannot take advantage of the expensive and sophisticated medical facilities in Lima, nor of its physicians. Consequently, we have devised a plan whereby we can prepare local women to give paramedical assistance. The plan is based on "modules" that comprise Basic Education courses sponsored by the Ministry of Education and it incorporates EDH's Child Development Program methodology for selection and training of volunteer participants; and previously-trained community health workers from the government's

Health Office responsible for the communities in which EDH's programs are located. In order to carry out the program, it was necessary to motivate and organize each neighborhood to participate in the building of its own "module" through a community work system. Women were selected from each square block or neighborhood committee as nominees for training. Centers for the Promotion of Women have participated automatically in those areas where the Child Development Program functions. In neighborhoods where there have been no EDH-developed programs, response by the residents has been noticeably less successful. In these cases, we have had to spend a great deal more time than was allotted to gain the residents' confidence and trust, and provide them with information.

Motivating "barriadas" to propose and accept their women in decision-making roles—whether as representatives to Community Associations, or as community health workers—requires patience and time. It especially requires that the program be carried out in such a way that it does not violate local customs or behavior patterns of individuals and groups. It took five long years before EDH could begin "phasing out" of the Centers for the Promotion of Women.

One of the ways we measure our success is by the degree to which women participate in community decision-making and become integrated into the structures of traditionally male-dominated associations. The other is when women understand their responsibilities and do not shirk them; when they know their rights and defend and demand them.

A RESEARCH EXPERIENCE WITH RURAL WOMEN

Isabel Chacon Acuna (Costa Rica)

In many ways, Isabel Chacon has lived two lives. The first began in San Jose, Costa Rica, as the daughter of Lucas Raul Chacon Gonzalez, lawyer and teacher; and Angela Acuna Braun, the first woman in the country to obtain a law degree in an era when educational opportunities for the feminine sex were almost nonexistent. Both parents, each unique in his/her own right, set the stage for the life Isabel is living. Her father was sent to Chile by the Costa Rican government to complete his studies, and was recognized as one of the country's first educators. Her mother initiated and directed the fight for womens' right to vote which was conceded in 1953.

Her parents sent her to Los Angeles, California, in the United States, to complete secondary school and to take a secretarial course. As Isabel says, "I didn't know I didn't want to be a secretary...it was the proper thing for girls from 'good' families to do...it was socially acceptable. The majority of Latin American girls in those days were raised in a very conservative, traditional system. Even though my parents each had a university education, they thought that being a secretary was an ideal occupation for a nice, middle-class girl."

Isabel returned to San Jose, worked as a bilingual secretary and administrative assistant for eighteen years. During this "first life," she also married and had two daughters, Laura Maria and Irene Maria. Hers was the role of the urban elite wife—fashionable, secure and enviable—dominated by custom.

Act II of Isabel's life began with divorce. A short time later, she entered the University of Costa Rica as a first-year student to study sociology. Although a novice to academic life, Isabel was a mature woman with some very practical experience behind her. Underneath her chic exterior lived her mother's daughter with all her concerns, ideals and values, determined to seek an identity of her own.

She threw herself into her study with a passion that was fueled by many years of suppressed intellectual curiosity and creativity. The university opened up her horizon onto a completely new world. The human and intellectual evolutionary process that occurred awakened her dormant interest in the effects of Costa Rican culture on its women, particularly low-income women and those with limited access to education.

Isabel began working as a volunteer with "The Integrated Feminine Labor Economics Development Association" (ASODELFI) while she was still a student at the University, in the belief that everyone should put their abilities to work in a positive effort to motivate and help others. Without such commitment, she believes there can be no progress in development or social change.

Isabel lives in San Jose with her two daughters, now sixteen and twenty years old, and her mother, Dona Angela.

27

A RESEARCH EXPERIENCE WITH RURAL WOMEN
by
Isabel Chacon Acuna

We were a group of professional women who had idealistically committed ourselves to the idea of developing women's self-awareness. We called ourselves "The
Integrated Feminine Labor Economic Development Association."[1] The group was
genuinely interested in how poor rural women felt about issues that were affecting
their lives and what their basic problems really were. We had decided to implement a non-formal education project for "campesinas" that could be used as a
basis on which to develop a model rural research study. Upon looking back, I
must say that while our approach was somewhat naive and Utopian, our intentions
were of the best. We didn't want to just sit around a table or at our desks and
speculate on "campesina" problems—no! We wanted to hear them from the rural
women, themselves—to get a response from the community.

Maria Cecilia Calero and I, professional sociologists, were appointed to design and
carry out the study. Ceci and I are from San Jose, the capital, and largest city in
Costa Rica. We both are university-educated and our lives and our circle of friends
revolve around an urban environment. Although our professional experience in
the rural areas was very limited, we nonetheless felt competent and academically
prepared to implement this rural development project. Our greatest concern was
that the area to be investigated be sufficiently close to San Jose so that we could
travel back and forth in a day, and not have to stay overnight to accomplish our
work.

The Province of Alajuela seemed ideal. It comprised twenty-two rural communities
and, depending on the weather, the trip from San Jose would take no more than
one to two hours by car. Of the twenty-two villages, we selected the community of
Concepcion as the base for the first phase of the project. Although relatively close
distance-wise to an urban center, it is extremely rural and in many ways, quite
remote. The main highway from San Jose will take you to San Ramon, a small
town that becomes a central point between many of the province's rural communities. From San Ramon, it will take another thirty minutes to an hour by jeep to
reach Concepcion over a climbing, twisting dirt road. The people of Concepcion
must depend on supply trucks and an occasional jitney or private jeep for transportation to San Ramon where they can catch a bus to San Jose. The
community's families are sprinkled throughout the surrounding mountains in tiny
huts on small parcels of land where they eke out a subsistence living from the
soil. Concepcion has two primary schools, a Health Center, and a Community
Development Association, all of which serve 210 rural families. The size of the
population of Concepcion, its proximity to San Jose and its community organizations would make it a perfect pilot for the eighteen-month study phase. We could
do all of our planning and preparation in advance.

---

[1]The Spanish name, "Asociacion de Desarrollo Economico Laboral Femenino Integral" (ASODELFI), is a
private, non-profit voluntary organization registered with the government of Costa Rica. It was founded
in 1977, to promote the development of women and the family through research and the dissemina-
tion of information, a specialized library, non-formal education and guidance, and volunteer work.

The purpose of the study as a first phase was to help us design a non-formal education project for women in all twenty-two of Alajuela's rural communities. Ultimately, we hoped that the project could be replicated throughout many rural areas in Costa Rica. We specifically wanted to take a close look at the effects of nutrition and environment on health; the opportunities for and advantages of education; attitudes toward family, labor and civil rights and responsibilities; education for family life; and opportunities for developing new kinds of productive activities, as well as improving those that already existed. It was a very ambitious undertaking, but as native Costa Ricans, we felt it was a necessary first step toward improving living conditions for rural women and their families. It could be a strong contribution to the progress of the country. We felt confident that as women working with women, our problems would be minimal because we would have immediate rapport.

The study would provide primary source data gathered first-hand from women themselves—not secondary source material from libraries, universities, government and international institutions. We would use group meetings and discussions as our main vehicle and tape recorders and other audiovisual methodologies, as well as questionnaires to gain our information. We spent weeks in preparing materials for slides, posters, audio-cassettes, and in designing the questionnaire. Being aware that the majority of the women were uneducated, we used the utmost care to phrase everything in the simplest language to make sure they would have no difficulty in understanding. At last, we were ready to begin.

The first step was to present the idea of the project to the women of Concepcion. Our approach was to introduce ourselves to the Sin Paredes Hospital in San Ramon which trains nurses' aides for rural health centers. Dr. Ortiz, head of the hospital, accompanied us to the Concepcion Health Center where he is well-known and respected. His sponsorship lent us credibility and was very important to our gaining the acceptance and cooperation of the community. He presented us to the Center's "nurse"[2] who had been trained at the hospital, and to the community women volunteers known as health monitors who assist her. They agreed to transmit an invitation to all the women of Concepcion to meet with us at the Health Center the following week.

On the appointed day, a mere fifteen women showed up. In retrospect, I think they probably came only out of curiosity and the fact that they had nothing else to do. Although we had prepared a number of posters explaining the project and had hung them in prominent spots around the Health Center, none of the fifteen women even bothered to look at them. It was almost as if they didn't exist.

The chairs were arranged in a semi-circle and we began the meeting with a verbal explanation of why we were working on this project, what it was all about, and how we would do it. On this latter point, we told them we would be using picture slides with a slide projector, group discussion meetings, instructive materials, and audio-cassettes with a tape recorder. The women, most of whom were between twenty-five to thirty-five years old, sat in silence. I couldn't tell if they were bored, disinterested, shy, or simply did not understand what we were saying. As one woman finally volunteered, "One is not accustomed to speaking in front of other people."

---

[2]While the people called her "nurse," in fact, the head of the Health Center is a professional nurses' aide.

We had brought along a tape recorder which we had placed in a strategic location to document what the women had to say, and we explained we were using it to make sure we would not forget or misquote what they said. But they didn't say anything. I began to be afraid that the only voices would be Ceci's and mine. It was extremely difficult to get the women to begin talking, but finally one—a mother of two little girls—hesitantly told us that her oldest who was ten, had been born with a harelip. "Everybody teases her and makes fun of her, even her father," she offered. *"La chita"*[3] has had several operations, but she still talks funny and doesn't want to go to school. Sometimes, the boys throw rocks at her."

The subject of the conversation about children aroused the interest of some of the other women and one by one, a few shyly began talking in small clusters to each other about their own families and problems. The tape recorder proved useless in documenting their conversations because it sounded as if everyone were talking at once. One could not distinguish anything intelligible.

Actually, the tape recorder at that meeting was worse than useless. Some days later, we learned through feedback from the nurse that the meeting had been a disaster. The tape recorder had raised great mistrust because some of the women had understood that we were recording what they said, to play back for the entire community to hear. One woman thought the tape recorder was a video camera and that she was going to appear on television like she remembered she had been sitting—in an unbecoming position with her hands folded over her protruding stomach.

According to the nurse, Concepcion had a history of negative association with tape recording. Some time ago, a community practical joker had taped a confidential conversation that took place in a discussion between a local woman and someone who was conducting social research. The joker then played the tape for the fun and entertainment of the men at the local beer hall. In Concepcion, where families are closely united by kinship, gossip about any member reflects upon the entire family. Any situation that would result in derisive gossip, such as the tapes played in the beer hall, would naturally trigger resentment by the family, as well as the victim. The community was on the alert for tape recorders from that time on and had great fear of being made to look ridiculous. In the light of their past experience, it is understandable that they were angry with us if they thought we were going to tape their voices and play them back for the entire community to hear. In our naivete, it had never occurred to us that they would be suspicious of us because of the tape recorder, especially after we very carefully explained its use in the program.

To our chagrin, we also learned that the women understood very little of what we talked about, in spite of the great care we took to use what we thought was the simplest language possible. It was not so much they they did not understand the words, but rather that they didn't understand their meaning. I was personally criticized because I spoke in a manner they interpreted as "uppity." My language was too fancy, they said, and they didn't know what I meant.

We found out later that the women of Concepcion average a third grade education and that they leave school principally because the educational system at the first and second grade level does not adequately prepare them to synthesize, evaluate,

---

[3] *"La chita"* is a regional pet name for girls.

31

or think abstractly. A questionnaire we later administered, revealed that 96.4 percent of the women read almost nothing with the exception of catechism.[4] The majority simply did not participate in affairs outside their own families and the home, received no stimulus from any other source, nor were aware of any possibility to change their situation or explore new opportunities.

Our experience with the first presentation was very disheartening. We were both frustrated and discouraged. All our great preparation had been useless and our self-assurance had been thoroughly deflated. I began to wonder if Ceci and I, two city women unaccustomed to the ways of country folk, would be able to sufficiently communicate with them to gather the information needed for the study, not to mention implementing the pilot project. We realized that we would have to redo the language on all the posters and revise the initial cassettes we had prepared. We would have to gain the trust of the women and attempt to undo the damage that had occurred by using the tape recorder at the first meeting.

The only possible way to achieve the trust and acceptance of the Concepcion women was to work at getting them to know us better and us to know them—to study and absorb their language and speech habits, to carefully observe the community, and to sensitize ourselves to everything about their reactions to us. We sought direct communication, but we had to improve our ability to communicate and make ourselves understood. We completely restructured our approach.

Because there is only one telephone in Concepcion, which is almost always out of order, our best opportunity to communicate with the women still remained with the Health Center nurses' aide and her community volunteers, and through Dr. Ortiz whom everyone loved and respected. The nurse knew everything about the community—not only the health and family problems, but the human element as well. She always knows who goes to school, who doesn't, what people do, who is getting married, whether they practice family planning, and who is feuding with whom over what. She and her volunteer health monitors became our most valuable advisors.

The health monitors are elected by the community at popular elections, so they are truly representatives of the people. In addition to collaborating with the Health Center and the community health committee, they also became our link to the youth committee, the sports committee, and the Association for Community Development. We invited the health monitors to become our first trainees and they agreed. We prepared a course especially for them based on the simplest formula for a workshop-type meeting. We wanted to train them to record and codify reactions to the messages we would present to the community women, as well as to give us feedback on how well the messages were understood, and the concerns and problems they aroused. Thus, the health monitors also became our representatives and guided the design and form of our research study.

The nurse kept a file on each of the 210 families in the community. Every family file contained an envelope with information about each of its members in addition to his or her entire clinical history and personal characteristics. The average family in Concepcion had six children. All together, they totalled 475 females and 518 males. Of the females, 398 were designated as women and the other 77, girls. It is a clan society and many of its problems stem from the fact that the majority of its

---

[4]Catechism is a summary of religious doctrine espoused by the Catholic Church, often in the form of questions and answers written in a manual.

population are blood-related; first cousins often marry. This may explain why there are so many cases of asthma, why the common cold is a constant, and why there is such a high incidence of fatal illnesses.

After our disastrous beginning, we instituted two changes that I credit with making it possible for us to continue. First, we annouced through the health monitors that mothers were encouraged to bring their children along to all future meetings. Secondly, at each meeting we asked the volunteer health monitors to explain the objectives of the project and the methodology we were using. From that time on, the number of women attending the discussions steadily increased. In addition to the mothers, our meetings at the Health Center were filled with their offspring— from infants to twelve-year-olds—and young women who were not yet mothers. Moreover, it greatly stimulated the participation of local women leaders, as well as assuring that our project was clearly understood. Sometimes, even men attended.

Gradually, as the women began to trust us and our motives, they seemed to become less shy, to openly participate in the discussion, and to expose their feelings. We were able to introduce the tape recorder again, not to record their conversation, but to test the trial cassettes we had prepared. Each dealt with a specific theme such as, "Bedwetting," "The Importance of Mother's Milk," and "The Disposal of Garbage," and were presented in the form of "soap operas" with dialogue between persons like themselves. They were extremely popular because, as one woman said, "They talk the way we do." We used the cassettes to stimulate the discussions and to present new ways of doing things that would improve their health and living conditions. We were able to explore, in depth, many of the issues that could not even have been mentioned earlier, such as attitudes toward sex. For example, we began one discussion by raising the question of the division of the boys and girls in playing games.

Two of the older girls who accompanied their mothers told us, "In the 'high school,'[5] the boys play 'futbol'[6] while the girls jump rope and play hopscotch. The teacher won't let us play games together because the boys are too rough and might kick us." We learned, however, that in the "lower school," there was no problem with the girls and boys jumping rope together, playing hopscotch and other games.

This discussion led to talking about the hope the women had for educating their children. There was no awareness or seeming desire on their part to orient their children toward vocational training. To the person, they all wanted their sons and daughters to go to secondary school, although they knew that given the problems of money, motivation, transportation and social custom, the chances for this were extremely slim.

The possibilities for Concepcion girls to go to secondary school are few. It was difficult to understand this at first because it seemed to me that the proximity of the community to the San Ramon secondary school and to San Jose, the capital, should have made it easier for girls to get an education. What I had not foreseen were the effects of fear and folklore used by the parents to control their daugh-

---

[5] The "high school" or "escuela de arriba," as it is called in Concepcion, is the seminary attended by the local students in the 4th, 5th and 6th grades, and is located outside the boundaries of the central community.

[6] "Futbol," which is directly translated as football, refers to the game of soccer.

ters. An example is one old Costa Rican folktale based on the story of a woman with the face of a horse who is supposed to appear at night on lonely country roads. As a result, the women of the community scarcely ever leave their homes after six o'clock in the evening. This made it almost impossible for girls to conceive of going to school beyond the local community. The limited bus transportation to and from the road to San Ramon would oblige them to walk, sometimes several miles from the bus stop, and would often preclude their getting home before dark. Women condemn themselves to live with this severe constraint on their personal development because they have been taught to be afraid, particularly to walk alone in the evening. The model woman is a good cook and mother who stays home and doesn't go out. The woman who is involved in clubs and such questionable pursuits as learning a trade or skill, at times is even considered a "tramp."

We found that not a single woman had finished secondary school. Although there is the night school in San Ramon, half an hour away by car, there are no women in attendance. In addition to fear of going out alone at night, they told us their parents would not permit them to go because there are male students, and because during the rainy weather the bus frequently breaks down. There was a strong implication that neither parents nor husbands trust their daughters and wives to be out at night alone or in a situation where they might be forced to walk, unchaperoned, with men, and thus bring their virginity into question. Mothers often excused themselves from continuing their education on the grounds that there was no one with whom they could leave the children.

The paradox is that while the ideal woman was seen as a good mother, and they

said they "always had to take care of the children," they admitted they didn't know how to do it very well. They knew they had to administer discipline, but were either over-tolerant or unduly severe in their forms of punishment, and commonly relied upon fear as a form of control. There are many ghost stories and tales of the supernatural that are perpetuated and handed down from generation to generation. A common technique is to say; "If you don't do 'such and such,' the *"tareco"*[7] will come and get you." No one knows for sure what the *"tareco"* is, but children tremble at the thought. Some say that it sounds like a great dog dragging its chains. Others describe it as a horrible-looking woman with a large cadaver-like head who has pulled most of her disheveled hair out by the roots. She always appears wailing and moaning on the banks of rivers where she is supposed to have drowned a child. Other traditional stories revolve around the cart that travels with neither people nor animals pulling it; and some are linked to religion, such as the one that keeps people from bathing during Passion Week because they might be turned into sirens. Women thus become victims of their own disciplinary techniques—participating in the exercise of social control, and creating the image of the ideal woman—by perpetuating fear.

We developed a tape cassette about "The Fearful Child," to help unravel some of the myths and misconceptions that we were encountering. Some of the children took an active part in the discussion, sharing their fears of certain animals such as cows and dogs. One little girl around ten years old, told about the time she found herself on a path in the woods, separated from her friends with whom she had been playing. Suddenly a man appeared who made advances, apparently with the intent of assaulting her physically. Now, if she has to carry lunch to her father when he is working in the woods, she feels like hairy arms are about to reach out from every tree to grab her.

Some of the women also remarked that they were terribly afraid of natural phenomena, ranging from earthquakes, thunder and lightening, to insects and worms. Costa Rican myths such as that of "the hairy hand"[8] have contributed mightily to their fears. There was a universal undercurrent of agreement among the women about their fears, and they, themselves, said that bringing them out in the open and discussing them was helpful. It made them aware that probably many of the noises they attributed to ghosts were no more than the natural sounds of animals which seemed louder and more frightening in the quiet of the night. Equally as important, it gave us the opportunity to observe the behavior and interaction between the parents and their children.

At the request of the women, we made another trial tape on "Sex Education" for discussion at the next meeting. We prefaced the playing of the tape with an animated cartoon film which provided an introduction to the subject. After we played the "soap opera" cassette, the meeting was opened for discussion.

A recently married young woman who had become quite outgoing, broke the ice. "My little sister had been asking me for a long time how to make a baby. I was never able to tell her because I didn't really know. When I knew I was going to get married, I decided to take a course in sex education they were giving in San

---

[7]A *"tareco"* has no exact word in English that serves to translate its meaning. It can be likened to a poltergeist, i.e., a ghost that rattles dishes, silverware and makes other noises to show its displeasure; moves things mysteriously from one place to another; or plays tricks on mortal beings.

[8]"The hairy hand" is a mythical figure akin to a bird, that makes a sound which warns that there is a lion or dangerous animal nearby.

Ramon—so, when she asked me again, I told her what I had learned. It wasn't at all embarrassing—in fact, it's really interesting how your body works."

Others in the group, stimulated by the young wife's frankness, began telling about the questions their own small children had asked, such as "Where do babies come from?" and the little boy who asked, "Why is my baby sister different from me?" All of the mothers found they were not prepared to give precise, simple answers and were usually embarrassed. In order to cover their embarrassment and satisfy the children's curiosity, they made up stories like, "Well, he came out of a 'pinuela,'"[9] or, "The stork brought her." When a woman is ready to give birth to a child, other children in the family are sent to stay with neighbors or grandparents, further shielding them from reality.

The open dialogue we were finally able to establish with the women of Concepcion on a subject as delicate as sex education was very rewarding. We knew we had been accepted and that this community of intelligent, although uneducated women—difficult to know as they were—regarded us with trust and affection. It also indicated that audio-cassettes as we were developing them, using the "soap opera" approach with fictitious plots and Costa Rican folk music interspersed with recommendations, sound advice and information, were a very successful vehicle for non-formal learning.

We were encouraged to try another very controversial subject, bedwetting. We made a cassette and then proceeded to test it at several different meetings, making corrective adjustments after each. Some of the reactions were very revealing. After having heard the cassette at two earlier discussions, one little boy about eight years old, moved a wooden bench into the center of the group, climbed upon it with great self-assurance and stated, "My little brother peed in his bed and mama really let him have it." The children tittered and the women chuckled appreciatively; the glances that were exchanged made me feel that many in the group were sympathetic to his mother.

Another child, motivated by the boy's spontaneity, stood up to speak. A girl of around ten or eleven, she told us she had wet the bed since she was five years old. She added, "...and my mother always beats me. She says I should be ashamed, 'specially since my baby brother who is only one year old has already stopped." With childish candor she continued, "When I 'wake up an' the bed is all wet, I get scared. I know she's gonna whip me, an' besides I am so 'shamed I hate myself. I don't know what makes me do it—I jus' wake up an' it's all done. Sometimes I hide the wet stuff under the bed so she won't see it an' try to cover up the wet places with dry things. She always finds it, 'tho..." and then the child sat down. The room was silent. No one knew what to say, but there was no doubt that the little girl had reached everyone.

The child's honesty seemed to give the mothers the courage to begin discussing the problems they had with their children and how they treated them. Almost all beat their children or used some form of corporal punishment, mainly because they didn't know anything else to do. When they began exchanging experiences after hearing the cassette, they began to question their attitudes toward their bedwetting children. The tape had dealt with the root of the problem and suggested several alternative ways of handling it. Above all, it caused them to examine their own attitudes.

---

[9]In Central America, a "piñuela" is the name for a tropical plant from which a coarse string is made. A type of cactus, it is also used for fencing.

At the meeting when we introduced the cassette on "The Importance of Mother's Milk," some of the attitudes that emerged could probably be traced to radio advertisements for condensed milk and the model women that some of the radio "soap operas" project. After listening to our cassette, one of the younger women commented that many didn't want to nurse their babies because they were afraid it would "make them ugly," meaning they didn't want their breasts to sag or lose their youthful shape. Another stated she knew several women who didn't breast-feed their children because they were too busy with other household chores.

Almost every time we met with the women, the subject of schooling would come up. The primary grade schools at the rural community level are very poor. The teachers are neither well-prepared nor well-paid. The women complained that the teacher did not live in Concepcion as the former one had done; instead, he commuted. He arrived in the morning and left at noon, giving very little of himself to his students. An ambitious man, he was studying school administration so that he could get a job with the Ministry of Education. We found this to be a fairly typical situation in the Province—one of the drawbacks of being close to San Jose. In some communities, we were told that when a teacher had examinations at the University, he didn't show up at all. In Concepcion, the women resented this and it had influenced their attitudes about the need to go to school.

Of the women interviewed during our study, 46.4 percent had had some schooling from the first to third grades; and 53.5 percent had attended classes in the fourth up to the sixth grade. Only 17.9 percent, however, had finished primary school.[10] One of the most consistent reasons for not concluding primary school given by 82.1 percent of those interviewed was that it was not as important as their duties at home. Many seemed to feel they learn more from the radio, and in some cases, television.

Most of the communities now have at least one television set. The rural women are enraptured by the Latin American "telenovelas,"[11] but they often serve to hurt more than help the uneducated "campesina." Most of these TV shows are "canned"—that is, they are made in other countries by companies who are in business to sell a product at any cost. They reflect life styles which are unreal and inappropriate for rural people in developing countries who have neither the money to buy nor any use for such products. Unfortunately, most of the women cannot separate the reality from the fiction. For example, one group of women recently was trying to acquire two typewriters. When we asked them why they wanted them, they replied, "Because the girls want to learn to type so they can be secretaries like the ones on television."

It took the full eighteen months for Ceci and me to complete the ASODELFI study, but by the time it was over I would have to question who benefitted the most—the women of Concepcion or the two city sociologists. It is true that our success with the experience has led us to expand the project to two additional communities in the Province of Alajuela. We will select new themes to develop with the aid of cassettes and continue to verify and adapt the original tapes to meet the genuine needs of "campesino" families. Most importantly, we developed a methodology for learning to interact positively and creatively with rural women

---

[10]Primary school comprises the first, through sixth grades.

[11]The "telenovela" is a short fictional story like the radio "soap opera."

and their families which could open up many new avenues to education for "campesinas."

Our greatest drawback was that in spite of our education we were not prepared to work in the rural areas, and we had had no real experience with rural culture and customs. This may sound odd since we were proposing to work in our own country where we had grown up, gone to school and lived all our lives. We had traveled from one end of Costa Rica to the other; after all, it is a very small country. But living the life of a "campesina," being one, understanding how they feel about themselves and how they feel about city folk like ourselves, is quite different. We look different, we dress differently, we talk "educated"—to them, we look "rich." Learning to empathize with the "campesina" was most difficult. It meant more than trying to understand how they might feel about us personally; it meant understanding how they had come to feel about elites who, for centuries, had been the "haves," while they and their families before them had always been "the have nots." It meant respecting them and earning their respect for us.

I am still learning and hope to continue doing so for the rest of my life. To a great extent in such a short time, Ceci and I were able to win the confidence and trust of the women of Concepcion. Without that, I would neither have been able to write this story nor to develop our non-formal education project which is now well on its way. Without their letting us into their lives, my life would still be restricted to the narrow view that keeps our countries divided and our women second-class citizens. It was a great lesson for this sociologist.

THE ONLY WAY

Ana Bleyswyk de Carlier (Peru)

Born in Holland of working class parents, Anita is the second of seven children. For as long as she can remember, she had wanted to become a nurse, but at the time she finished her secondary education, she was too young to meet the age requirements for acceptance. Instead, she was allowed to study to become a medical analyst. She learned first about centralized, automated and technically-equipped hospital laboratories, but found them to be cold and sterile, their scientific precision lacking in compassion, human warmth and understanding. The only difference she could observe between a highly-automated factory and a modern clinic was the sign over the entrance which announced it was one or the other.

At the end of her training as a medical analyst, she sought employment in an institution that was more in line with her concern for human beings. Thus, she began her professional career in a small hospital in Amsterdam where she could become personally acquainted with the patients and follow their progress. It was while she was working at this small hospital that she met a young male nurse with whom she fell in love and married. She admired him greatly and from him learned many of the important aspects of nursing. Together they secured work at a psychiatric hospital. Little by little, as she began to understand the mentally disturbed patients, she learned to love them. She studied their values, their ways of thinking and feeling, and concluded that the majority were simply victims of our "dehumanized modern life."

As this "detested" modernization took over even the small laboratories, Anita became more dissatisfied. "Each year they budgeted for more and more equipment. After a while, all they will need are monkeys to turn on the machines," she protests, even now.

Unfortunately, about this time, her marriage came to an end. She and her husband had followed separate paths of personal development which ultimately drew them apart, ending in their separation and finally, divorce. During this period she paid a heavy price for the emotional dependence she had allowed herself to place on this man, and suffered greatly in the years it took to free herself. But, as the pain gradually subsided, she began to rebuild her life according to her own values and beliefs which she was just beginning to discover.

In these days of introspection and self-searching, Anita joined a group called the "Small World Project," where men and women helped each other find new life styles and search for improved social objectives. The Project investigated alternative food habits, organic gardening and appropriate technologies. The group helped Anita to clarify and resolve her own ideology, reinforcing her growing belief that the roots of the inhuman system she had witnessed in hospitals and laboratories—"the suffering and deaths are merely statistics used to feed computers"—grew out of exploitation of the masses, their lack of employment and the general miseries of human beings and countries.

The Project was also responsible for introducing Anita to her second husband, Hans Carlier, a young agronomist who shares the life she discusses in her article, *The Only Road*. Hans had formerly been a volunteer in Kenya and they had known each other only three months when he was offered another foreign assignment as an agricultural volunteer with the Agricultural Society of Social Interest in Peru. He postponed accepting the offer until he could convince Anita to accompany him; meanwhile, having been presented the idea, they both prepared themselves for the possibility of living and working in this new land. They studied Spanish and innun- dated themselves with all things Latin American—books, music and food. Anita at- tended a short course on "development problems," got acquainted with some Boli- vian refugees, and reorganized her thinking to include more attention to natural foods. She laughingly says her friends upon learning of their plans to move to Peru, "sympathized with something like compassionate admiration, as if I were a martyr planning to sacrifice myself for the savages."

Although she was almost certain she could deal with her new life, there were moments when she feared the reality might be more difficult than she could imagine. She continually reminded herself that she was a very practical and resourceful per- son, that she could take care of herself, and that hardships did not intimidate her. She knew she could sew, cook, play a musical instrument, relate to children, and that she understood nursing and about natural foods.

She was impressed during her first weeks in Peru by the startling contrasts and inequities. "House-sitting" for a wealthy Dutch family taking a vacation provided the Carliers a place to stay that was filled with lovely hand-crafted works of art, antique furniture, books, and "many rooms which a servant constantly dusted in spite of the fact that they were always clean." But Anita was unable to ignore the misery of the people in the street that could be observed "from any window in the house." As she searched for another place to live when the vacationing family returned, she in- vestigated both wealthy and impoverished neighborhoods. Poor and rich alike told her, "We will rent to you because you are a "*gringa*.""[1]

If Anita found Peru full of contrasts, she also found it brimming with opportunities to practice her own beliefs. She could hear the silent cries for help louder than if they had been shouted from the hospitals, women's prisons, nursery schools and employ- ment agencies for domestic servants. She began preparing herself for the volunteer work to which she is now dedicated. One can suspect that Anita has chosen work as a volunteer because it reinforces her conviction that woman must work to free herself and, as a volunteer, she alone takes the responsibility for her decisions along "the only road."

---

[1] In Peru, the term "*gringa*" or "*gringo*" connotes a fair complexion usually associated with European and Northamerican ancestry.

THE ONLY ROAD
by
Ana Bleyswyck de Carlier

Facing us on the dirt floor as if we were in two separate worlds with a line drawn between, was a small group of rural women, many of them barefooted. The social worker, a Peruvian woman with obvious academic background, was charged with making the presentation to the women. She referred principally to the "generosity of the functionaries of SAIS who," she said, had "spared no effort" to bring them a foreign horticultural specialist and put him at the service of the communities. "With the knowledge of this expert," she added, gesturing toward my husband, "you will soon be growing vegetables of a much better quality and as a result, you will be able to get higher prices at the city markets."

At that time, having just completed my first five weeks' residence in Peru and with but a few hours in this rural community of the Central Sierra, the social reality of the region seemed an impenetrable enigma. Notwithstanding the fact that my knowledge of the language was rudimentary, the general meaning I gathered from the social worker's words greatly surprised me. I was even more astonished when she severely admonished the women for their poor attendance at the meeting.

"Unfortunately, you're a miserable group," she lashed out at them. "Look at how few of you are here—what a disgraceful showing! You are incapable of appreciating the enormous effort that we make to come here! You aren't interested in anything. And I'm practically certain that not even one of you knows what SAIS is. Let's see—does any one know what SAIS is? S-A-I-S!" Contemptuously, she spelled it out. No one opened her mouth. "See! Not one of you knows, even though your husbands all work at SAIS! SAIS means the Agricultural Society of *SOCIAL* Interest....!"

It took a long time for me to understand why the social worker was so insensitive, and to learn the reason behind the women's lack of interest and poor attendance at the meetings. The presence of a few tired and hungry-looking souls undoubtedly had some significance, although at that time, neither my husband nor I were in a position to comprehend.

Then came the speeches of the technicians with whom we had travelled to this village—self-important and academic despite their false tone of kinship with these poor rural mountain folk. The technicians or so-called "experts" included a sociologist, an accountant, a male nurse and lastly, my husband.

At the beginning of the meeting, my husband had suggested, "It's not the right time for me to speak. I don't know anything about the community's problems yet, nothing of their experiences, their ways of thinking, their possibilities...."

"That's not important," the other technicians responded in unison, "You're an expert, aren't you—you certainly can speak about your own *specialty!*"

Left without an argument, he had no choice but to improvise a quick lecture to satisfy our companions. With the aid of a few graphs and drawings he put together on the spur of the moment to supplement his poor Spanish, he managed to make his presentation tolerable.

The women facing us were busier breast-feeding their babies, cleaning their bottoms, and quieting their crying, than listening to the lectures. Others were simply half asleep with nodding heads or yawning in boredom, fatigue and hunger. I later learned of the long, hard days these women spent laboring both in the fields, and in the home. They sow, tend and harvest the crops side by side with the men, herd and care for the animals, spin and weave the wool, wash and mend the family's meagre clothing, cook, care for the children and perform innumerable other chores. At the time, I was unaware of these realities, and it seems now that the technicians must have always ignored them.

Our visit to the community was scheduled for one day only. Following the meeting with the women, the nurse dedicated himself to selling antibiotics and vitamin tonics, and to painting with mercurochrome the many infected surface sores he was able to catch sight of—activities which apparently made him feel indispensable and satisfied. The sociologist busied himself gathering statistical data from the local school which he surely must have felt would enrich his reports and which, no doubt, confirmed his theories. The accountant ran into "serious problems" trying to correct a deficiency in the account balance of the consumer cooperative because he had lost his electronic calculator. My husband and I spent the remainder of the day getting acquainted with the town. We strolled through the village and ended up in the vegetable garden of the community's highest authority where my husband was pressed into giving a horticultural demonstration.

The department of SAIS to which we were assigned had arranged a dizzying trip for us to become acquainted with many communities. In practically all of them, we encountered more or less the same dynamics. At the end of the tour, the department admitted that the program had faults and indicated they had decided to change their strategy. The changes planned were not related to such real issues as paternalism or that the program provided only superficial assistance without getting to the root of the problems; instead, the concerns were over the high cost of gasoline and per diem. In the future, they planned that the technicians would remain a minimum of six months in each region, beginning with the Valley of Canipaco. My husband was assigned to Chongos Alto, a centrally-located community among eight other member communities and three Production Units.[2] SAIS, in Cahuide, functions like a cooperative, serving a total of 28 "campesino" communities and seven Production Units—approximately 4,500 families.

The majority of the production units are economically well-developed livestock farms that prosper as a result of their superb location in the region's grassy highlands. The local communities, on the other hand, barely subsist. Like stubbornly rooted vestiges of ancient "campesino" struggles against Peru's successive colonizers—from the conquistadores and their heirs, to contemporary transnational corporations—they persist, half-hidden in the shadows of the narrow valleys or precariously clinging to the steep rocky mountain-sides.

---

[2]"Production Unit" is the name the former military government of Peru gave to the old "haciendas" (ranches) which were confiscated under that government's Agrarian Reform policy. The "Production Units" were then made available for purchase by the "campesinos" through the "Agrarian Debt" program.

The "campesino" families work their small parcels of poor land with beasts of burden, hand-made implements, and human willpower. Their meagre harvest is mostly destined for family consumption and limited bartering at regional markets.[3] The men supplement the family's small harvest by working as part-time labor at the mines, jungle and coastal plantations, production units, and in the cities.

Although the community accepted us with kindness and put a small plot of land at our disposal where my husband could begin his experimental vegetable garden, many questions and uncertainties troubled me. Would we be accepted by people of a culture so different from our own? Would our being foreigners present an impenetrable barrier to knowing these people? Would we be able to cope with such hard living conditions? And what about the language problem that, under certain circumstances, could turn a simple attempt to communicate into a dramatic encounter? How could we discover our errors in time to avoid repeating them, and above all, where were we going to find the vision and the foresight that would be indispensable to making a worthwhile contribution? It was certain that no matter how carefully we planned nor how much we wished to help, nothing would succeed except those things we based on our experience here in the community. To this we dedicated ourselves with enthusiasm.

Early on, we found that we were never alone. At first, the villagers carefully kept apart, and only the children timidly came near to ask curious questions. Charged with caring for their younger siblings, they came carrying the little ones on their backs, placating their cries with boiled potatoes stuffed in their pockets for the purpose. It was not long, however, before we had as spectators a few women who watched us from a prudent distance, protected by a wall. Little by little, the space between us seemed to get shorter. The passersby increased and I had the feeling that many of the same people were walking by several times a day to look at us, always taking quick sidelong glances but never stopping. Gradually, the more audacious stopped to openly observe our work—then, a few men and schoolboys overcome by curiosity, gained the courage to enter our yard. Almost without realizing it, we found ourselves engaged in difficult but delightful conversations with them.

The women did not actually venture close until the first harvest of our experimental garden. But when they finally came, it was not only to chat, but with a more practical scheme in mind—that of leaving us potatoes, beans and "mashua"[4] in exchange for a cabbage or a head of lettuce.

"Why are you doing these things?" they asked, referring to the garden.

"To find out if these vegetables can be grown here," we would answer. "Many people claim they can't be grown here because the soil is poor, the sun is too hot and the nights too cold. We're trying to find out what's true and what isn't."   ·

"Sounds like a good idea," they would comment. "Lots of 'em [technicians] come and all they do is talk, nothin' more. But you folks're working just like us. That ain't bad!"

---

[3]These open-air markets called "ferias" are usually a weekly occurence held around the town square or in an area specially designed for the sale of items produced by the local community.

[4]"Mashua" is the Quechua name for a plant with an edible starchy root similar to a potato.

Or, "I got a little piece 'a ground and would kind'a like to try it, too. You got any seed left you can spare?"

And when we gave them the seeds they would ask us to show how we had cultivated them. Thus began the first demonstrations and thereafter, communication continued increasing. We became acquainted with more and more people who continuously sought to discuss their experiences with us—their mistakes, their successes, and the possibilities. Relations expanded and grew a little closer each time.

By this time, my Spanish had improved a little, but many of the women spoke what seemed to me a very indistinct mixture of Quechua and Spanish that I was simply unable to understand. I strained to repeat their words without much success, entertaining them greatly and making them laugh. I deeply felt that what they appreciated more than the linguistic playfulness was the human touch. Our contact was more than merely a fresh, spontaneous exchange of congenialities and opinions; it went much deeper than that—it was as real as life itself. They would touch my arms, compare their hands with mine; they even braided my hair, as if they wanted to make sure that I, too, was a human being just like themselves.

I discovered their diet was very simple and that they only ate onions, cabbage and lettuce sporadically, usually when they went to the village. They soon began to learn from us about other vegetables whose seeds, seedlings and cuttings we sold to them at cost. The women asked me to teach them how to cook the vegetables, and so I gave demonstrations in the village "plaza"[5] where they were able to sample the results. "Mishki," they would say in Quechua, meaning "very tasty."

I never selected dishes that they would not know how to prepare; rather, I incorporated the new vegetables into their traditional recipes. They learned to replace the "yuyu,"[6] which grows only between February and April, with Swiss chard, cabbage, carrots, endive and spinach. The children and babies especially liked the new recipes and began begging their mothers to get the new vegetables.

This reaffirmed my conviction that promoting the cultivation of new vegetables alone was not enough; I also had to teach them how to use them. I was even more convinced when women I had not seen before came around to ask me to repeat the instructions for preparing a new recipe. Thus it was that I began to be invited to their homes to participate in the preparation of meals which they shared with me. This gave me the opportunity to transmit to them my own knowledge through simple advice and practical recommendations, and help them to assimilate good nutritional habits like the eating of grains and cereals with vegetable soups. At the same time, I was able to warn them about the dangers of insecticides and of eating processed foods with negligible or no nutritional value such as white bread, pastas and bleached rice.

Through these experiences, I realized I had discovered a valuable process. I had been admitted to the most conservative and traditional sector of the community, but certainly not the least important—that of the women! The organization of farm production in these communities rests primarily with the women because the

---

[5]"Plaza" is the Spanish word for "town square."

[6]The Quechua name for tropical colewort.

men are forced to migrate, seeking to sell their services to bring home needed extra pennies. The long absences of the men, together with the prohibition of owning their own draft animals—all oxen, horses, burros and the like were converted to use by the Production Units—forces the women into manual labor. To ease their burden, my husband constructed models for a grain sifter, a thresher and a hand plow which could be made easily by community carpenters.

In addition to doing the farm work and caring for the home, the woman organizes all family life and sells at the local market whatever part of the harvest is not essential for family use. She is commonly victimized by "middle-men"[7] who take undue advantage of illiterate, rural women, their lack of knowledge about marketing and money exchange. These local merchants, for the most part well-to-do "campesinos," are able to purchase the best harvests when prices are most depressed. They then sell these foods back to the communities when they are scarce and prices high. Through the markets, they are able to control the economic life and social organization of the communities, which always results in their election as local authorities. Consequently, they own the largest grazing lands and best cattle, aside from the Production Units.

One day, several "experts" arrived from a government ministry to give short courses for the "campesinos." These technicians invited me to participate, but I felt it would be wiser to just observe. I watched the disinterested faces of the women when the nutritionist explained to them hour after hour, chart after chart, about vitamins from A to Z. I observed her expression of exasperation when one of the women stood up and said, "That's very nice, 'Senorita,' that there are so many kinds of food to nourish us, but tell us where we can buy these proteins and vitamins that you are talking about because around here all that we can find are potatoes, wheat, barley, beans and peas."

For me, these words "turned on the light." Now, I saw that it would be necessary to begin discussing with the women their own traditional food plants and link them with more practical demonstrations. From there on, I dedicated myself to searching for herbs and wild vegetables, and begged the women to bring me all of the different ones they knew and used. I also solicited the help of an old woman known as "la curiosa,"[8] who was reputed to heal with herbs. It was not long before I could speak knowledgably about the nutritional and medicinal properties of most of the common plants. Thus, I both learned from the women and taught them, passing on the information I gained from some to others, and teaching the preparation of home remedies. I was innundated with questions as the women pinched and sniffed the herbs. Some mentioned other lesser-known plants, many with Quechua names which I noted for investigation and possible incorporation into future demonstrations.

Little by little, the women began trading information and teaching each other. Soon a kind of epidemic arose in pursuit of knowledge about nature. In this way the women realized that their common herbs, garden vegetables and wild plants contained the famous vitamins that the nutritionist always spoke of. The discovery amused them greatly.

---

[7]In Latin America, the "middleman" is the person who buys the raw product from the producer and resells it for a profit to the consumer.

[8]"La curiosa" literally means "the curious one," but in some regions of Latin America, particularly rural areas, the term is used in reference to a "healer" or "witch-doctor."

With experimentation, they learned to cure colds with garlic and onions, diarrhea with carrots, anemia with prickly nettle and spinach, fever and flu with common watercress. They also perceived that some vegetables not only alleviated pain but were useful in preventing illness. In addition to the nutritional, curative and preventative properties related to one's health, they began to understand the economic advantages provided by these humble herbs in contrast to the expensive commercial products sold by the town pharmacist, the male nurse with SAIS and other public health advisors.

Not everything went smoothly, however. I had to struggle to overcome popular misconceptions promoted by public advertising and salesmen. For example, one teacher had spread the idea that one or two drops of chloromycetin in each baby bottle would prevent diarrhea. Another is illustrated by one woman's comment, "I have plenty of breast milk but I prefer to give canned milk formula to my baby because they say it's better."

"How can it be better," I questioned, "if on the can it states that milk made from the formula only 'approximates' mother's milk?"

Many of the women shared their problems with me. "I have suffered terrible hemorrhaging—once I almost died," one confided. Another said sadly, "My baby died from diarrhea and vomiting. My other children all have it, too." Others questioned, "I have so little milk—why is that?" "Why is it that my children always die? Already I have lost eight." "Do you think I have some kind of sickness? My head aches constantly and I feel so weak."

The thing that alarmed me most was the women's resignation to the death of their children. I constantly tried to persuade them that the high rate of death among their little ones could be avoided by changing some of their harmful dietary practices during pregnancy and later, with their babies. I struggled to demonstrate that certain home remedies could overcome diarrhea. In this often uphill battle, I frequently encountered responses such as, "But sometimes it is their time to die," and "But if it is God's will....?" Such replies really tested my patience and I would counter by attacking their fatalism. In an attempt to make them reflect on their duties as parents, I reminded them of the inability of babies and children to care for themselves, and of their own responsibility to protect these fragile lives by seeking ways to improve their nourishment, avoid illnesses or cure them.

I began to see the need to speak personally with pregnant women, and mothers of babies and small children, so I started giving short courses on pregnancy and child care. I began by giving a demonstration on the preparation of a home remedy for diarrhea. Later, I made friends with the local midwife and became her helper, assisting with deliveries and treatment of the newborn. I admired her for her broad practical knowledge; she could tell precisely what was happening inside, the minute she touched the belly of a pregnant woman. She knew exactly how to guide the fetus into the birth canal by shaking the mother in a blanket. We laughed together, celebrating the happy deliveries; and cried over our failures like the woman who left her newborn baby out in the night cold so it would die.

"Poor little woman," the midwife commented, "when her man comes home, he beats her, leaves her pregnant, and then takes off again."

At that time, I was working completely on my own. Shortly thereafter, the officials of SAIS were prompted to offer me a paying job. An optimistic projection indicated about 20% of the people in the Production Units were affected by tuberculosis; my task was to confirm the figure. My experience in Holland as a medical analyst qualified me to undertake the study and the local health clinic had the necessary laboratory equipment to carry it out. I accepted their offer, but withdrew from the commitment almost before I began. The social worker with whom I was to collaborate, did not provide me with the necessary information for the time period to be investigated; and the people in the Production Unit emphatically refused to furnish samples of their saliva for the tests!

"What're you going to do with my spit?" they asked, declaring, "...it's part of me, it contains my soul."

I knew that if the statistics indicated a high rate of tuberculosis as a result of malnutrition and the prevailing miseries, as they surely would, my efforts would be much better spent continuing with the nutrition courses and preventive medicine. It was then that I fully accepted my role as a self-appointed educator without institutional ties or support.

After this, my contacts with the community women became even more frequent and intimate than previously. The time coincided with the period of less work which follows the harvest, making it possible to spend more time with them. It became a daily habit to visit with them and exchange ideas—ideas which now went beyond nutrition and health concerns. They had begun to allow me into their private world of complex problems.

In the "old days," the relationship between the rural man and woman was more equally balanced and based on the division of labor. Although the heavy work with draft animals was reserved for the man, the woman helped with all agricultural chores. Community life was preserved by ancient ancestral practices of reciprocity. Now, however, as a result of the government Agrarian Reform program, life for the poor "campesino" has changed, not always in his favor. Unfortunately, it favors the woman even less.

The fundamental objective of the Peruvian Agrarian Reform is to seek the integration of the "campesino" society into the national society; or in other words, to integrate the "campesino" population into a market economy with all the relevant changes in values and social behavior. This has meant an unfavorable situation for the rural woman. Some have continued to work alongside their husbands as shepherds for the Production Units, but only the man receives a salary, meagre though it is. During crop crises, many of the paid shepherds lose their jobs. If the woman has been working at her husband's side, she seldom has anything to cushion the hard times ahead.

The daughters of the pastoral families are obliged to help with the herding and consequently spend many years of solitude in these lofty bleak regions, learning to speak only Quechua. When the girl gets married, she is required to live in the village of her husband and often has a very difficult time adapting to a new family and unfamiliar surroundings. Many girls are becoming aware of the empty future awaiting them and are rebelling.

"I don't want to be like my mother and sisters who began having children when they were fifteen! After that, they were pregnant all the time! I don't want a husband who is only interested in giving me more children, unless he leaves me!" But when these young women seek their own fulfillment, there are but two roads open to them: seasonal farm work for others—or, employment as domestic servants in the cities.

The difference in the way the family treats their sons and daughters is notable! The boys are regarded as an additional source of labor, a help, and even an economic asset. Girls, on the other hand, are separated from the boys and are considered only of help to their mothers who, themselves, are viewed as little more than slaves. When girls terminate their schooling, if they are fortunate enough to get any, they are still expected to remain at home under control of their parents.

One girl told me, "I would like to study, be a teacher, or a nurse—but my father does not agree. He thinks it's useless to spend money educating women who are going to end up taking care of children and cooking anyway. He says, 'We have to save so your brother can study. When he becomes a professional, he will help you and support you.' And now my brother is an engineer, and I am still working in the fields, still helping Mama, still taking my crops to market. Men have proposed to me, but I don't want to marry someone who will beat me, fill me with babies, and always be drunk like my father because he can't find work."

The growing problem of rural migration to the urban areas, and the high birth rates in rural communities have worried national authorities for some time. In 1978, the government put into effect an emergency program designed to "space" pregnancies. The objective was to put in place 10,000 interuterine devices or coils in six months. All field nurses were required to attend a special course to learn how to insert the coils.

Our local nurse in Chongos Alto was indignant. "'Campesina' women don't even know how their own bodies function—they should be taught that first. Then if they wanted to avoid pregnancy, they could choose a method they liked." She put together some pamphlets and gave talks to men, women and high school students of both sexes.

My close personal contact with the women made it possible for me to deal with these problems on an intimate basis. The fact that I had no children and did not get pregnant made me, by simple deduction, the community's most experienced person on this subject.

The problem one woman confided in me was typical. "My husband works in Lima, and when he comes home we have problems because I don't want any more children. He says I don't love him and that's why I don't want sex. But that's not the reason. He doesn't make me feel any pleasure, he's the only one that enjoys it. He wants to take me to Lima, but I don't want to go. I was in Lima once for two years working for a family. I had to do everything—cook, wash the clothes, clean the house, take care of my children as well as those of the mistress, do all the shopping and account for the money she gave me. I didn't get any salary: they paid me with old clothes for my children and myself, with meals and a little room on the roof. I don't want that life again. We work hard here, too, but at least what we do is for ourselves. I tell my husband that I don't want to die like my mother of an abortion, and I remind him that everything in the city is much more expensive—clothes, shoes and school. I remind him that we are poor and that life in Lima is no good for the children."

The girls told me about their sexual experiences, which were almost always unfortunate; the problems with contraceptives and their lovers; the lecherous abuse by their male relatives. "When they [the relatives] are drunk they grab me. Since we all live in the same house, there's no way I can escape."

Even many of the young men came to me with their problems. "I've gotten my girlfriend pregnant. I feel bad because she's worked so hard so she could study...I don't have any way to support a family, and I am studying, too. Now that her belly is starting to grow, they'll catch on at school and she'll be expelled." Usually there is no penalty for the man, but often his conscience bothers him if he is fond of the girl. The young woman is the only one who is condemned by society.

I received them as friends and after listening to the stories of their dilemma, I usually suggested that they discuss the situation openly with their girlfriends and try to come to some mutual decision together about what they were going to do. If they returned to me together, having considered all the alternatives, and had finally concluded they could not marry and raise the child, I would agree to speak to the midwife who arranged for adoptions and abortions. It always presented a traumatic decision to be made with no experience and with no one to whom they could go for sane advice. Thus, in addition to giving practical demonstrations on nutrition, raising vegetables, preparing them, and the medicinal use of herbs and wild plants, I now found myself adding meetings for students to discuss such topics as sexuality, "machismo" and responsibility. These meetings were all endorsed by their teachers.

By this time, it had become clear that practical demonstrations and informal discussions by themselves were not enough. The community also needed a simple handbook they could use as a home reference to guide them. This resulted in *Good Nutrition and Health for the Entire Family*, a manual I put together using their own vocabulary. It contains all the information we covered in the discussions, demonstrations and experiments, including recipes and home remedies.

After four years in this sierra community, my understanding of and relationship to "campesino" problems, particularly those of the women, has convinced me that genuine economic and social development can occur only within a framework of freedom from oppression. It must come from an integrated process directed at satisfying the material necessities and spiritual needs that spring from the heart of a people. Indispensable to its cultivation are self-awareness and self-reliance. It must also take into consideration the ecological limits of the land and structural changes of the society at all levels. The results should make possible collective, but equal participation by all the people in the economic and political decision-making process.

The "campesina" is destined to play a major role in freeing the rural society from oppression: first, because she has been the greatest victim of the Peruvian social system; and secondly, because of her proven capacity to struggle against impossible odds, and her humanitarianism. The only road to freedom will be long and difficult, with many hurdles and pitfalls. She will have to unite with her sisters and wage an organized battle against the cultural traditions which oppress them—against the family and social structures that have enslaved them—against the poverty, the attitudes and the indignities which degrade them. Her two most efficient weapons are awareness of her present status and the will to change it; and self-education, an instrument which can be invaluable if honed to a sharp cutting edge.

Although I come from a different culture, my efforts will never cease to be directed toward building a better world for our sisters. My hope is that the reader will join us on this, the only road.

LEARNING TO TAKE HOLD OF
ONE'S OWN DESTINY

Carmela Moor de Crespo (Bolivia)

The oldest of four children, Carmela Moor de Crespo was born in the southern State of Tarija, a Bolivian mining region. Her paternal grandfather came to the area of Sucre from Europe as a professor for children of the wealthy mineowners. Carmela grew up in the shadow of the mines where her father worked for Jochi and Aramayo as an engineer for 35 years.

Because there were no schools at the mining camps, Carmela was sent as a boarding student to the *"Colegio"*[1] *Santa Ana*, a Catholic school in Tupiza (State of Potosi), the town where her mother was raised. After finishing both primary and secondary grades at *"Santa Ana,"* she returned home to the mining camp. Hers was a family that adhered to the belief that women were best suited to be housewives. Her father, a very traditional-thinking man, was caught on the horns of a dilemma. He could not allow Carmela, his favorite child, to work at the camp; but, at the same time, he agreed with the prevailing social custom that girls who had finished boarding school should return home for at least two years. This notion interfered with Carmela's burning desire to study at the Normal School. For as long as she could remember, she had always wanted to be a teacher and her mother tried desperately to influence her father, to no avail. In the end, it was always the man who made all the decisions and Carmela's wish was not fulfilled. When the appropriate two years at home had expired, she succeeded in convincing her father to send her to Argentina to an institute that specialized in "technical" studies for young ladies, such as pattern-making, sewing, embroidery, crocheting and tatting, and china painting.

It was during this period that Carmela met the man who was later to become her husband. Also a Bolivian, he had secured a position with the Central Bank close to the Argentina border. They were married shortly after she finished her studies in Argentina and are now parents of three grown children, a daughter and two sons. She has tried not to repeat the pattern of her father, whose traditional ways had such an impact on her life, although her husband too, opposed her working when the children were small. "I managed to keep everyone moderately happy," she states, "by adjusting my working hours to conform to the family needs."

In 1968, she met Father Roberto Melchior, a Belgian diocesan priest, who was in the process of establishing the National Center for Integrated Learning (CENAFI) in La Paz. Carmela worked with him in the beginning as a teacher of technical skills, and two years later when he returned to Europe she became director of the center. Since then CENAFI has been the pivot around which her life revolves.

---

[1]The equivalent of "grade school," it can include either or both primary and secondary grades.

Perhaps the most important single event in her professional career, one that has had visible influence on her work, occurred in 1974 when she was selected by CONEPLAN[2] (Bolivian government) to receive a 3-month fellowship to study in Israel. The program, sponsored by the Organization of American States and the Government of Israel, sent thirty-four fellows to Tel Aviv where they studied all aspects of the Israeli national development program. Each of the Latin American countries was represented except Chile and Argentina. Carmela was one of only four women in the group.

Now retired, her husband is fully in accord with her beliefs and the work she has committed herself to. He often travels with her to the *"altiplano"*[3] to help in establishing her dream, a regional rural center for underprivileged *"campesinas."*

---

[2]National Planning Council (English translation).

[3]The *"altiplano"* is a series of high plateaus in the Andes where the elevation ranges from 12,000 to 13,000 feet above sea level. Most of the eastern part of the chain is dry, hard and stony, except during the rainy season when the clay gives way to mud. It includes the area of Lake Titicaca that produces rice and the major part of the country's fish. Most of the year is bitter cold and windy. Many of the villages are remote, and the inhabitants have neither water nor electricity.

LEARNING TO TAKE HOLD OF ONE'S OWN DESTINY
by
Carmela Moor de Crespo

The Bolivian class structure imposed by colonialism has preconditioned our society to oppression. Its existence often causes us to believe that woman should play a subordinate role. It is easy to trace the origin of this thinking and observe its development side by side with the oppression that engulfs us. It acts as a barrier to changing the system that dictates our lives and it will not disappear until the class structure disappears. The only way women can achieve emancipation will be to support and give strength to each other and to collaborate with other oppressed sectors that also fight for equal rights and access to the goods and benefits of our heritage. Most importantly, we must not align ourselves unconsciously with any of the sub-systems within the system based on class structure. Neither must we succumb to the capitalist consumer system that imposes goods and services that we don't need and can't afford, and which are inconsistent with our culture and our way of life. And lastly, we must never subordinate ourselves to the yoke of the male who proposes to dominate.

Let me state from the very beginning that in Bolivia, I do not believe we can afford feminism as such. We cannot afford to isolate ourselves or to polarize our country between men and women. Bolivia needs now, more than ever, the common effort of both sexes to throw off oppression. The liberation of the Bolivian woman is the liberation of the Bolivian man. It is the liberation of Bolivia itself.

Although the structure of the classes is like an old tree and seems firmly established in Bolivia, its fruit is drying up. It needs to be uprooted. I believe we must seek new trees—alternative systems—that are more appropriate to our soil. This is why non-formal education is directly tied to women's struggle for emancipation, as well as to the national search for liberation and social change. Young trees produce better fruit.

At the National Center for Integrated Learning (CENAFI), in La Paz, an average of 2,000 people—mostly young women—pass through our classrooms each year. Our objective is to equip low-income and illiterate women with the tools they need to cope with life. The women who come here do not have to know how to read or write; the doors are open to everyone. Contrary to formal education, we do not require them to have this or that prerequisite or to pass any examination prior to entrance. Formal programs are based on specific time schedules which rule out attendance by women with family responsibilities and those who must work to eat. On the other hand, CENAFI's objective is to equip low-income and illiterate women with the tools they need to cope with life.

Someone once said that in order to move forward you should be totally conscious of your reality, to be able to understand those things which affect you daily and what choices are available to you, and to be aware that you alone are responsible for your actions. I agree with this statement. It is a statement born out of knowledge. It is a statement that says, "I am capable of taking hold of my own destiny." At CENAFI, we work to achieve similar goals.

One of the areas that has personally concerned me is the area of education as it affects our women; and more specifically, how the lack of understanding and in-

54

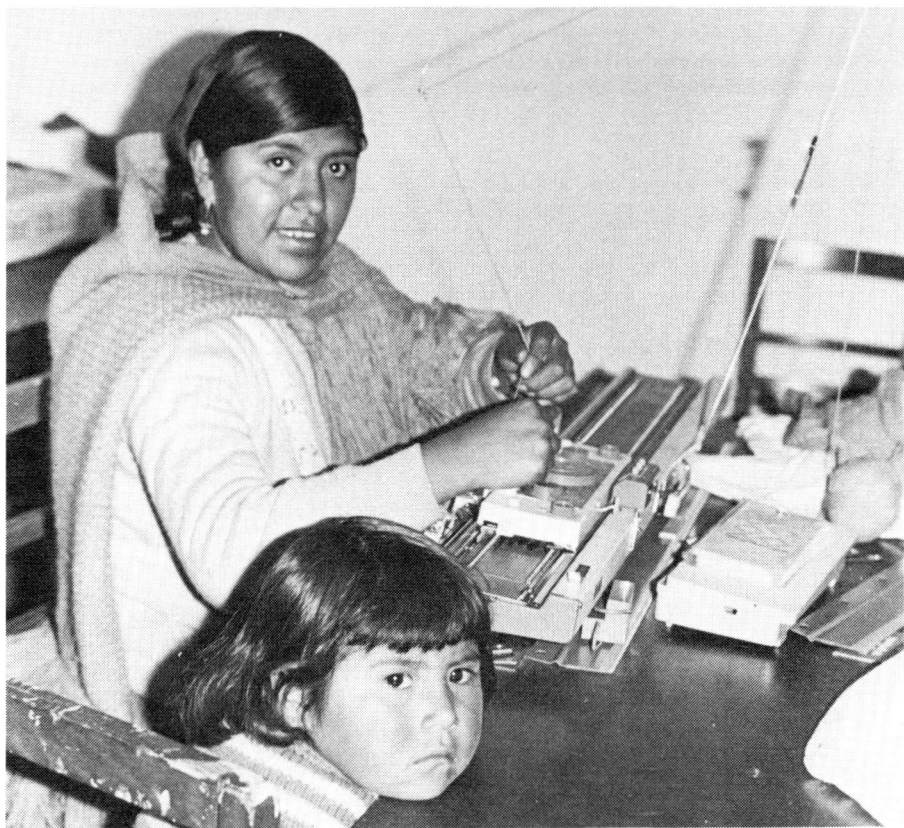

formation chains us to oppression and the belief that we must subordinate ourselves. When I am in the rural areas and see young women who have a pressing
need for information about life beyond their village, girls who have such desires to
learn—yet for whom there is no one to impart such knowledge—this is what
drives me to continue, often against what seems like impossible odds. CENAFI is
the place where, as director, I feel I can do the most to meet this challenge. I will
be content if one day I see that in some small way I have contributed to the ability
of the "campesina" to overcome the forces that have prevented her from taking
hold of her own destiny.

The Center, as its name states, believes in integral learning as an answer to the
development puzzle. In the twelve years since we were founded, thousands of
women have passed through our classrooms: around eight to nine hundred each
semester. Last year, we had more: twelve hundred each semester. This is possible
because the Center is open from 9:00 A.M. to 9:00 P.M. every day, Monday
through Saturday, and we handle three groups of students each day. From 9:00
A.M. to noon we offer courses for urban women who are not working, and housewives who must be home to prepare the mid-day meal and care for children who
are returning from school. Classes from 12:00 noon to 5:00 P.M. are attended
mostly by our live-in students and women who work only in the mornings. A
small percentage of our evening classes which run from 6:00 P.M. to 9:00 P.M. are
attended by men, most of whom are enrolled along with women who work during
the day. Our live-in students of course, can attend all three sessions. The Center is

really for those who need it most—the poor, the worker, the *"campesina"*—and by keeping it open from nine to nine, even those who have to work in the daytime can still come at night. In addition we have a kindergarten for pre-school children of our students which makes it possible for the mothers not to worry about their little ones. The children basically learn things on a smaller scale that their mothers are concentrating on.

Although we have a large number of students from La Paz, most of our women come from remote communities. They leave their families to spend a six-month training period in La Paz where they live at CENAFI because of the distance and lack of transportation to their villages which are mainly in the *"altiplano," "valles"* or *"yungas."*[4] The rural communities from which they come, elect these young women as community leaders, and raise the funds to send them to CENAFI in La Paz. CENAFI provides scholarships which cover the costs of food, lodging and all expenses of instruction for the full six-month period. The only condition under which these young *"campesinas"* are elected for scholarships is that when they have successfully completed the six-month course, they must return to their communities and teach to others what they have learned. In most of the villages, no one can afford to pay anyone anything, so the returning students must work as volunteers and provide their own food. Staff from CENAFI continually visits the volunteers during this time, providing them with advice, assistance and support. After several months working in their own communities, they return to CENAFI again, to take more advanced courses. At the termination of the scholarship, each woman receives a diploma. When they return the second time to their villages, they are encouraged to organize three-month courses, seminars and other projects for groups of local women. What they have learned in La Paz is adapted, comple-

[4]See "Editor's Note" about Bolivia at the beginning of "Integrating Women Into Rural Cooperatives: Pluses and Minuses" by Bambi Eddy de Arellano.

mented and improved by application in the rural areas. In addition, the groups are becoming part of a rural network which enables us to disseminate information in remote areas where it is impossible for communities to raise the money to send people to La Paz.

I also want to add that while poor rural women are our principal concern, we do not limit ourselves to helping only the "campesinas." As I said earlier, we try to reach women at all social levels, both urban and rural, because we believe that all levels of our society suffer from the social system imposed by the class structure. The Bolivian woman, as do most Latin American women, suffers from double oppression: first, as a woman; and secondly, as a working woman. As a woman, she is seen primarily as an element of sex and reproduction. As a worker, she is seen almost entirely in the role of the housewife. She, herself, maintains and perpetuates the system, reinforcing it through a series of biological mechanisms over which she has little control. I am generalizing, of course, but nevertheless I believe that these two factors affect all Bolivian women.

For example, a recent census stated that only 22.8% of Bolivian women participate actively in the country's economy. This figure reflects how women see themselves, as well as how they are viewed by men, since only the persons who are heads of families participate in the census. It also indicates the devastating effect of performing daily chores which are taken for granted, particularly if we look at the masses of women whose families stay alive because of the woman's work. By day, the "campesina" labors in the field alongside her husband, and at the end of the day, must take over the household chores of caring for the children, cooking, doing the laundry, nursing the sick and aged, and making clothes for the family. The capitalist system under which we live regards this as no more than every woman's obligation to her family, as a wife and mother, and for which the only remuneration should be her own satisfaction. But let us also look at the urban dweller—the city-worker—the domestic servant, the store clerk. Is her situation different? During the regular workday, she works X number of hours at a job which she is glad to get because work is hard to find and unemployment is high. She usually finds employment only for work that men prefer not to do, that is, mostly for jobs that are traditionally "women's work." Regardless of the number of hours required, she is generally underpaid. If she has a family, she plans to care for its members "after working hours," and for this there is no remuneration. "After all," it is said, "that is her responsibility as a woman."

At CENAFI, although the majority of our students are working women—both rural and urban—we do not exclude women who have greater economic means. We have been criticized for opening our courses to those who are not among the needy but I strongly believe that we must, at all costs, avoid class distinctions. Raising the social consciousness of women from higher income levels is essential if we are to change the condition of social stagnation which provides the framework on which our class structure is based.

By now, you must be wondering just what it is that women come to CENAFI to learn. We concern ourselves with everything that has impact on women, everything that affects children, young people and mothers of families. Our courses are semi-technical, what is generally considered non-formal education.

Most of our students from La Paz speak two languages—Aymara[5] and Spanish.

---

[5]Aymara is an ancient Andean language spoken by most of the rural people who live on the "altiplano."

Sometimes those from the *"campo"*[6] speak only Aymara, and for these we have Aymara-speaking instructors who teach them to read and write, beginning with learning how to measure both in Spanish and Aymara. In this manner they begin their "integrated" learning. Understanding how to read directions is integral to learning how to get along, to taking care of yourself in this world. At the same time, they learn to measure, read directions, and to apply these new skills to the courses they have elected to take.

The rural students bring to CENAFI six or seven subjects they want to learn about in accord with the needs of their home community and region. They then choose the classes that to them seem to best meet these needs. Let's say cooking, for example. When they return home, they are able to improve the meals for their children and improve their own diets when they are with child. Moreover, they will understand why they should eat corn and drink milk, and the role that vitamins play in their health. If they choose pattern-cutting and sewing, it is usually because there are several small children at home. They cannot afford dressmakers and wish to learn how discarded clothing can be recut and adapted for smaller sizes to ward off the bitter cold of the *"altiplano."* All our courses have their special significance for Bolivian culture, and each one complements the other.

One area of CENAFI's curriculum includes what we call "feminine orientation." In spite of the fact that we also accept male students, the majority are women. Feminine orientation is really an adjunct to our other courses on an ad hoc basis, and responds to needs the women discover in themselves, as a result of their other classes. We urge them to answer simple questionnaires and to suggest subjects about which they would like more information, apart from those they

---

[6]*"Campo"* is the term commonly used in Spanish to refer to the rural áreas.

brought with them from their communities. CENAFI then contracts with specialists in the areas requested, to come to the center and give talks, seminars and discussions. They have covered a wide range of interests such as drug addiction, psychological problems and family planning.

We offer a number of practical courses that will have a lasting impact on the lives of the women who come to CENAFI, and their families. Classes in reading and writing, first aid, knitting, pattern-cutting, sewing and tailoring, home improvement, health and nutrition, cooking and cooperative development are directly related to family and community life. What they learn in these courses can be applied immediately to improving the quality of life in their villages and urban "barrios."[7] Classes in baking and dessert-making, carpentry, machine embroidery, machine knitting, cosmetology, barbering and hairdressing, mechanical and manual arts, and electric installation and repairs, are more popular with our students who live in La Paz who must earn income and compete for jobs. Surprisingly, however, there is a good deal of crossover of interests which is part of the plan to integrate the students. In many of the rural villages, money is scarce or nonexistent, so competing for jobs is not a reality. Nevertheless, it is important for the rural students to understand the problems of living in the city and vice versa.

Courses traditionally for men such as carpentry, mechanical arts, electrical repairs and cooperative development are open to all and we find they are attracting more and more women. Last year, a woman—a mother of three children and expecting a fourth—enrolled in the carpentry class. She wanted to open her own carpentry shop. By the end of the course, she had made all the furniture for her living room, as well as a very attractive dining-room set. Who is to say that such courses should be reserved for men or that women cannot excel in these traditionally male fields?

I have observed that the biggest handicap for the rural woman is that she lacks knowledge about the world outside her own village. She does not lack intelligence. Often her community will have a limited, or no source of water and no electricity. She gets up at the first light of dawn and goes to bed when she can no longer see. I doubt that she ever takes a complete bath, as we think of it. Perhaps she can wash her face, hands and feet in a stream if one exists, but when water has to be carried long distances it becomes very precious. Few of these remote villages have any sanitary facilities. The woman who comes to CENAFI for the first time arrives with her bowler hat and her "manta"[8] filled with all her earthly belongings, often including a small child. The impact of the city can be terrifying! The world of CENAFI seems upside down—everything is totally different. She has to sit at a table to eat and we have to help her learn to manage her food with a knife and fork. Personal cleanliness can be a big problem. It is not unusual that she may never have seen a toilet that flushes, let alone understand its use.

During the first week at the center, we usually notice that the women, particularly those from the "altiplano," are very reserved. It is difficult to get them to say anything, and when we speak to them, they hang their heads, shrink or cower. Past

---

[7] "Barrio" is the common Spanish word used to refer to "neighborhood," usually meaning a low-income area.

[8] "Manta" is the name of the homespun cloth, usually woven of wool, from which the rural women make large shawls. The shawl is used to carry packages, food, babies and other goods, as well as to provide warmth.

experience has taught us that the only way we can help them to integrate and open their eyes to alternative life styles is by gaining their confidence. We dedicate ourselves to this. I, for example, show them how to lie on a bed and explain the use and need for bedclothing. I show them how to use the bathroom and frequently find myself demonstrating the correct way to sit on the commode and what to do with the toilet paper. I have to emphasize that the commode is not to be used for washing clothes or the hands, face and feet. Once we have earned their trust, their shyness disappears. They relax and become very open, freely discussing their needs and concerns.

The results have surpassed our wildest dreams. These women have returned to their villages, having resisted the seduction of the city. They have faithfully taught others in their communities and these, in turn, have reached the most incredibly remote spots. But I am not going to say that we always have a smooth operation —on the contrary, we have faced a number of problems.

When the women return home, we find that they sometimes have difficulties with their communities. Not all have the same calling. Some of the "campesinas" have very strong personalities and a certain innate will to dictate. They sometimes reason, "Now that I have lived in the city and have received special training, I am better than the other women in the village." They occasionally become confused when the same people in the community who chose them to go to CENAFI, now reject them. We spend a great deal of time helping them to overcome this attitude, and explaining that the community selected them to go to CENAFI so that they could return and share what they have learned.

It is very important that they reject instead of mimic the example set by our traditional social structure; in other words, the example of the upper classes who dictate to the underprivileged. We try to instill in them that they are not "better than" the others in their villages—they have had only more advantages—and that these advantages are a result of their selection by their communities. We stress that these advantages do not entitle them to be waited upon; but rather that they now have a great responsibility to share their learning.

My own special interest is to create several rural centers similar to CENAFI in La Paz. We have a very modest beginning of such a center in the "altiplano" at Aguachaca, about 133 kilometers from La Paz. It will be a regional center where the "campesina" will not have to suffer the strong cultural shock of going to La Paz. In this way, we plan to prepare her in advance for the impact of the city, and then bring her to La Paz for advanced classes later.

The Aguachaca center is called the Center for Professional Training, and is headed by Father Toribio Porco, a young Bolivian priest, who is the new pastor of the church at Sica Sica, a couple of kilometers away. Local alumni of CENAFI make up the staff and are being paid small salaries so they can give their full time without penalizing their families. I have been spending part of each week at Aguachaca in order to reinforce Father Toribio's efforts. We hope that before long we will be able to raise a few small animals and plant an experimental garden, but there is a great deal of work yet to be done there. In spite of the fact that we already have the first class of fifteen students in residence and the need for the center is overwhelming, scarcity of funds make it impossible to move any faster.

Although CENAFI is completely self-supporting, the greatest barrier to our expansion in the rural areas stems from a chronic condition of inadequate funds. It is like a throbbing headache which can be dulled with a little aspirin, but always comes back when the aspirin wears off. We live with the realities of this limitation.

As opposed to most other private, non-profit voluntary organizations, we receive no funds from the government, from any foreign entity, nor are we affiliated with any other institution which provides financial support. The ancient building we occupy is lent to us by the Archbishop. Our income is almost entirely from the tuition paid by our urban students. We receive a small return on the crafts that we export to Europe which are produced by the "campesinas" while they are learning, and this covers the cost of the materials utilized. We earn a bit of money from the room and board we provide at a very small cost to a few young women who come from the rural areas to La Paz to study at the university and normal school, but who have no other place to live. Although CENAFI is registered with the Government of Bolivia as a private, non-profit organization, we must pay import taxes on all imported equipment and materials used by the center, as well as export taxes on the craft products we send to Europe.

In spite of these handicaps, I am forever optimistic. A fundamental part of this optimism is my belief that what we are accomplishing at CENAFI in our program for the "campesina"—in our efforts to integrate all kinds of knowledge into their lives, to broaden their perspective and their alternatives—will make a difference. I don't want to lose sight of the fact that this is only one facet of the "integration" that will be necessary to change our social structure. But it is a component, and a very important one. Taking hold of one's destiny must go in hand with and be reinforced by support for integration at all levels. Integration can provide the cord that ties our society together. It must replace the class structure which tears us apart.

OUR NATIONAL INFERIORITY COMPLEX:

A CAUSE FOR VIOLENCE?

ABOUT THE AUTHOR

Ana Audilia Moreira de Campos (El Salvador)

Ana Moreira is well-acquainted with the departments[1] of San Miguel, Cuscatlan, and Sonsonate in both the eastern and western parts of her country. She was born on September 9, 1937, in the village of Chinameca (San Miguel) at the foot of the volcano for which it was named. She attended the primary grades in her home town, then went to Izalco (Sonsonate) to study at the Rural Normal School from which she was graduated as a teacher. She later took additional courses at the Holy School in Cojutapeque (Cuscatlan), then returned to earn a diploma in Arts and Sciences from the "Liceo" of Chinameca.[2]

Many of Ana's courses were oriented toward religion, and Christian ethics became a prominent interest in her life. After graduating from the "Liceo," Ana joined several clubs in Chinaco that were linked to the rural diocesan centers. In 1973, as a result of her skills and leadership, she was appointed to work with Sister Alicia Erikman at the Guadalupe Center which had been recently established in San Miguel, capital of the Department of San Miguel. Together they developed the idea of training a network of rural women to teach others in a self-generating cycle which could multiply and attract new members as it grew stronger.

Ana became director of the Guadalupe Center in 1974. In the six years of its *"campesina"* program—from 1973 to the writing of her article—Ana has been involved in training 895 rural women from every part of the country. She has had an unusual opportunity to witness problems and hopes of *"campesinas"* of all ages, and her article is principally based on information they shared at the center during the week of their training that concentrates on self-awareness and "personal development of the woman."

Ana loves her people. Because she is in daily contact with the suffering that ignorance causes, she constantly worries about the future and what it portends for El Salvador. She believes that women must play a much more active role in decision-making if violence and brutality are to be overcome.

Ana is married to Jose Adan Campos and was expecting a child at the time she wrote, "Our National Inferiority Complex: A Cause for Violence?"

---

[1]The equivalent of a "state" of the United States.

[2]A local secondary school.

OUR NATIONAL INFERIORITY COMPLEX: A CAUSE FOR VIOLENCE?

by

Ana Audilia Moreira de Campos

Editor's note: *This is a heartfelt commentary by a rural woman in El Salvador who is representative of the disenfranchised masses. It is imperative that we listen to this spokeswoman, for her voice carries a message that the world must hear. Her rendering of a basic social ill in El Salvador cuts through to the heart of the massive social and political problems confronting her nation today.*

As Enrique Dussel[3] cogently states:

> *...the common woman is the real basis for the process of change in society. She has a message that we must understand. It is quite different from the one we would hear from a woman of the upper levels of the power structure.*

> *It is necessary to listen to these women as though detached from the system and not as oppressed by it. This distinction is essential, because it is one thing to support a strike in order to buy a new refrigerator. That is simply wanting to get rich with the rich. It is something else to search for a system in which equality is real.*

> *Therefore, we must listen, but we must know to whom we are listening. We must hear the often murmured protest which is not part of a feminist movement, and know that the desires of the masses are usually expressed in distinct and simple words.*

In innumerable ways, the greatest problems of Salvadoran society lie between men and women—not between the political factions of radical and reactionary. Political upheaval, although endemic to our nation, is a sensational release for emotional turmoil that begins in the home. Men subconsciously seek physical violence as an answer to all problems, whether they be in the streets, against their political opposition, or with their wives and children. Violence and inhumanity in our country has become a way of life.

Life is especially difficult for our rural women. Living conditions are extremely harsh. Health and nutrition are only as good as the quality of the water, food, and sanitary facilities, all of which range from poor to non-existent. All the good land for farming is owned and operated by a small oligarchy that is politically committed to keeping things just as they are. With so little of the land available to the small farmer, the rural people are dependent on the mercy of the landed few. Because of this, men who earn little or no income have almost nothing to be proud of except their virility. They have few ways to relieve their frustrations, so women often bear the brunt of their discontents.

---

[3]Enrique Dussel is a philosopher and historian from Argentina who takes equality of man and woman seriously and can be trusted by us when he tells women how to achieve liberation.

There is absolutely no respect for the human dignity of women. It is common for their husbands and fathers to beat, kick and humiliate them in the most vulgar ways. They act ashamed to be seen in public with their wives, sisters or mothers, as if it would make them seem less manly among their friends. Much of the Salvadoran man's free time is spent competing with his cronies for the attentions of casual girlfriends to prove their masculinity. The tragic results are unwanted, illegitimate children.

The majority of men in our rural communities refer to women as "idiots," "pigs," "worthless," "disobedient," "deceitful," "disloyal," "lazy," "stupid," and "daughters of whores." A man most often thinks of his wife as an expensive burden because she eats and consumes food that would otherwise be his. If it suits his mood, any of the above perceived qualities serve as sufficient reason for him to mistreat his wife.

The story is as old as my country. From the day she is born, a female is regarded as inferior. The birth of a girl child is a great disappointment: the father is disappointed because his friends will think him less of a man, because now he will have another worthless "mouth" to feed and because he cannot count on a daughter to earn him income. The mother is disappointed because her husband will think less of her than he already does because she could not make him a son. The daughter is disparagingly referred to as an "hembra," the word used for female animals, and she is treated accordingly from then on. No one is joyful, for there is nothing to

be joyful about. No one celebrates the birth of a girl; instead, the parents consider that they are in for trouble and many headaches.

On the other hand, when a boy is born, they say they have "won the prize," or "hit the jackpot," and they celebrate for days with all their friends. If the father has a gun, he shoots for joy and gets drunk in the village. No one condemns him because *he* just had a son. If it was a girl, it was the wife's fault; if it is a son, he takes the credit. The male child is not referred to as a *"macho,"* a male animal, the counterpart of *"hembra."* Instead, he is respectfully called a *"varon,"* meaning a human being of the male sex. The midwives long ago noticed this difference and very shrewdly charge more when a boy is born than when it is a girl.

As he grows up, a boy is carefully taught not to cry. He is constantly reminded that "only girls cry, not men." If a boy gets into a fight, it is a matter of family pride that he must win. If he loses, his father wants to know why. "You are a man —next time you must hit harder!" is the usual rejoinder of a father whose son has caused him to lose face among his peers.

It is accepted that boys have freedom to come and go as they please. Girls, however, are not allowed to stray from the family plot. They are told that women are meant to stay home, that they are in danger outside. Parents tell their daughters that if they leave the house they will get a bad reputation which will dishonor the family name. So girls stay at home and learn to carry out all the household chores which will perpetuate the myth of their inferiority to better serve their domineering fathers and future husbands.

The plight of rural housewives in El Salvador is especially discouraging. Caring for a house and children is hard work—especially if the house has only a dirt floor, is open to insects and rodents, has no electricity or water, and no latrine. The daily preparation of breakfast, lunch and dinner for a hungry family means long hours over a hot fire or coals. It means grinding corn and making *"tortillas"*— but, it can also mean making something out of nothing. Being a housewife in the *"campo"*[4] usually requires scrounging for firewood; feeding and caring for the animals—pigs, chickens, whatever—and sometimes taking them to market; caring for the children and doing the laundry; mending the clothes; and carrying lunch in a pail each day to your husband, wherever he is working. Depending on the circumstances, this can mean several miles.

[4] *"Campo"* is the common term used to refer to the rural areas, and is the word from which *"campesino(a)"* is derived.

Because few rural homes have water, *"campesinas"* carry the family laundry to the nearest stream or river where they beat the clothes on the rocks with home-made soap to loosen the dirt. Some of the larger villages have a central well and a community sink with cold running water where the women both wash and fill huge jugs to carry home for drinking. The woman's job never ends. She has to work at least sixteen hours a day to complete her chores. She is invariably the first up in the morning and the last to go to bed at night. Only the very rich women can afford to do otherwise.

Men, however, think women's work has little value. They say you can't see women's work—that it provides no money for the family to live on; therefore, it cannot possibly be worth as much as the job of a man. As one *"campesino"* told me, "Women are able to work in the shade where it is cool and comfortable. A man must earn his living by the sweat of his brow in the heat of the sun."

Some women are now beginning to realize that this argument "doesn't hold water." Women work at least twice as long as men every day, Sundays and Holy Days included. There is no time off to drink beer, gamble, play "futbol" in the road, or meet with friends—except possibly over the laundry. Many are aware that it is mainly through their efforts that the body and soul of the family is held together. A tremendous amount of time is needed to keep the small business called "home," working—or as is sometimes said, "make ends meet."

Men, somehow, overlook these basic facts—or choose to ignore them. Most prefer to believe that women fritter away their time. A sufficient amount of male unanimity on this score, of course, serves to "keep the wife on her toes," striving to do better. Little girls are taught very early that the main thing they are supposed to do is "please" the menfolk, and they grow up to spend their lives at this thankless and impossible quest. Friction and strife in the *"campesino"* home continues endlessly because it is the only way the man can maintain his feeling of superiority.

In our society, men control almost every facet of life. From the government to the Church, from political parties and cooperatives to sports, men run things. They make the decisions about what's good and what's bad. Women have become the nation's beasts of burden, shouldering the basic responsibilities of the family and society in order that men may be free to pursue whatever work and pleasures they desire. If husbands, fathers and sons are involved in violence outside the home, which has also become a way of life, the women suffer equally. When men are wounded, bruised and lacerated as the result of the terrorism which has held our country in its grip, women faithfully patch them up and nurse them as best they can with pitifully little knowledge of first-aid and no medicine, only to see them go and involve themselves in fighting again—maybe the next time to be killed. But, it is not for the woman to question why. She has no say in any of the affairs that may leave her homeless, widowed, and at the mercy of the violence which surrounds her. Every day this problem grows worse.

The participation of women in the social and economic order is restricted to serving and taking orders. They are never allowed to make decisions of any consequence. Although women now have the right to vote, it doesn't mean very much. They are told how to vote by their men. Social and political comments and opinions of women are made fun of or "put down." Any attempt by women to alter their situation is quickly censured—by government, family, and social pressure.

As a result, Salvadoran women are confused about who they are and their status in society. They are led or driven to believe that men are superior, that they are worth more. Women have been taught that men have more rights and there are daily examples to prove it. One woman I know who was very young and already had six small children, each a year apart, told me the doctor had said she should not have any more babies or else she might die. He suggested that she use some form of birth control. Confused and worried, she sought advice from her local priest. He told her not to worry, it was very simple; all she had to do was to practice "rhythm" and to abstain from having any intimate relations with her husband during the crucial ten or so days after her menstrual period. Her reply was, "Yes, Father, I will try again, but I am not sure it will work. I mean, it works very well for me—but it doesn't work at all for my husband." The poor woman's dilemma was obvious. We are taught that men are our masters—they command and we must obey. Many women have even come to see men as more like God, which is contrary to all Christian tenets and makes no common sense at all.

This myth of women's inferiority continues to flourish because of traditional customs and educational biases that have conditioned both sexes to believe the male is superior, both mentally and physically. This national inferiority has been created and forced by men. Institutionally, it is maintained and reinforced by the school system, the government, the Church, the community and the family.

It is up to the women of our country to take it upon themselves to change this humiliating condition. One way we can do this is by carefully developing our aptitudes and abilities, then using them to assert ourselves. There are a number of things we can do if we make up our minds that we must have equal rights and responsibilities at the same time we share our lives. The responsibility, however, lies with us.

As director of the Guadalupe Center[5] in San Miguel, I head a program especially designed for women. We train and sponsor groups of rural women catechists[6] who work in their own communities to make other *"campesinas"* aware that each is an important part of the society in which she lives. We try to help them become an integral part of the community, and to understand their rights and responsibilities. As human beings and as Christians, women have to struggle for our God-given right to equality. This is the only way for *"campesinas"* in particular, to rise above the sin of ages-old oppression for which men, historically, have been responsible. Resolution of the problem must begin in the home, so we take a grassroots approach. Our *"campesina"* catechists live in their communities and are on the spot to tell others about our program and share the information they learn at the Center. Their closeness to the other village women makes it possible for them to help those who are interested to come to the Center for training, too.

The kind of training we give always revolves around improving the lives of rural women; this is the core of the program. The training is implemented in courses of fifty-one ten-hour days in which the women learn about leadership, health, reading and writing, Christian rights and responsibilities, prayer, the history of El Salvador, the family, self-awareness and community organization. We also introduce

---

[5]A private, non-profit, voluntary organization, created to advance the cause of Christian ethics and equality for women in rural areas of El Salvador. It was established in 1972 by the Campesino University of San Miguel.

[6]The term "catechist" is used as the name to describe the community volunteer social workers who are dedicated to a Christian point of view.

Christian ethics through studying women of the Bible, the history of liberation, the true Christian man and a general introduction to the Bible.

At the termination of each course, the women return to their communities to put into practice what they have learned. After six months, we follow up by visiting to see how they are getting along and if they need any additional help. The parish priest is also very helpful in passing along information. They hold community meetings to generate self-awareness, as well as meeting with individual women in their homes where more personal dialogue can take place. The *"campesina"* catechists are dedicated to the promotion of change in our rural institutions, especially the schools. In this way, we are informing our children at an early age that men and women have equal rights, and that everyone can make valuable contributions to the development of El Salvador.

The sad reality of violence and brutality in El Salvador is a tremendous source of concern for all of us who do more than simply reflect on the struggle by women for liberation. We are all human beings—not animals! God created all of us with equal rights. I do not believe He intended that half of humanity be disparaged, controlled, manipulated and subjugated.

The *"campesina"* catechists, along with many others in El Salvador, are committed to the eradication of ignorance which has led to the complete oppression of women by men, and to the brutality and injustice which is sweeping over the country like a tidal wave. Our commitment will help to create a more just society of which all our people can be proud.

September, 1979.

**ONLY YOU MEN
HAVE YOUR NEEDS SATISFIED**

Luz Vicenta Luzuriaga Najera (Ecuador)

Luz Luzuriaga is a very serious, concerned woman. Professionally trained as a secretary and a journalist, since 1969, she has been the director and moderator of a radio program, "Women's Issues," broadcast daily from Riobamba by *"Escuelas Radiofonicas Populares del Ecuador."*[1] Riobamba has always been Luz's home, as it was her mother's and grandmother's before her.

The Luzuriagas were a humble family of *"campesino"* heritage rooted in the Province of Loja located at the southernmost tip of the country. Luz's father was a day laborer in Riobamba, a man who was able to attend only the lower grades of primary school. Her mother had no formal schooling to speak of, but possessed an overwhelming ambition for her five children to acquire an education. The struggle to overcome the handicaps poverty leveled on them was difficult every step of the way, but Luz completed her secondary education at the "Santa Mariana de Jesus" High School. She never knew what it was like to go to parties because their economic situation did not permit any luxuries or frivolity, only study. Given the circumstances, she has achieved a place in the social system that by every indication was completely beyond her reach.

Luz believes that part of the reason she has come such a long way is due to her parents and their commitment to values which made a lasting impression on her life. From them she learned to recognize her own priorities and then to search for those things she deemed most important. Her father continually quoted a Biblical maxim, "Scrutinize everything, omit nothing; all is good."

In addition to having a poorly remunerated but somewhat steady job, her father worked on the side as an artist and as a writer. From him Luz learned to sketch and paint, and used vacations and any free time to contribute to the family income by working in his studio. All the children had to help earn the family livelihood. Her father and brothers took care of all business dealing with the public, such as clients, commissions, and other affairs; Luz stayed "protected" in the studio. Her mother, concerned that she was becoming introverted and afraid to meet people, insisted that she look for work outside the home. She secured a job as a cashier for a small business in Riobamba where she worked for six years, giving her the opportunity to meet many workers. It was here that she began to understand the need for cooperatives and *"campesino"* unions.

---

[1]"Ecuadorian Radio Schools for the Masses" (English translation).

Her interest in the development of cooperatives and unions led her to many courses and seminars on the subject, some of which enabled her to travel beyond Ecuador to such places as Argentina, Peru, and Mexico. She began spending her spare time as a volunteer worker for a local savings and loan cooperative federation. This did not please her employer; consequently, she lost her job as a cashier and was unable to find work for two years. In the meantime, she continued working with local cooperatives.

Luz began working with *"Escuelas Radiofonicas"* as the result of their assistance to a small cooperative she was helping to get established. Her first position was as secretary to the organization. In addition to directing the program, "Women's Issues," she has served as the Secretary General, as well as coordinator of their Tele-Education Program, and editor of the women's section of their bilingual newspaper, *"Jatari."*

In January 1981, upon the death of Father Ruben Veloz, Director of *"Escuelas Radio- fonicas,"* Luz was appointed to take his place by the president of the institution, Mons. Leonidas Proano, Bishop of Riobamba.

ONLY YOU MEN HAVE YOUR NEEDS SATISFIED

by

Luz Vicenta Luzuriaga Najera

Editor's note: *In 1972, Ecuador's military government passed an agrarian reform law that gave private landowners until January 1, 1976, to cultivate eighty percent of their farmlands or face expropriation. The law did not result in any pronounced increase by the large landowners in making their cultivable land productive. Despite the January 1 deadline, however, only a few thousand acres were actually expropriated and turned over to land-starved peasants. The situation was particularly serious in Chimborazo Province. In May 1976, Jonathan Kandell wrote for the New York Times:*

No land distribution has taken place around Canton Colta, an attractive fertile valley in the shadow of snow-capped Mount Chimborazo, the highest peak in the country...About 30,000 Quechua-speaking Indians live in the valley, whose land and politics are dominated by 5,000 whites, almost all of them of Spanish descent.

'The authorities think the Indian is stupid, lazy and that he doesn't know his rights,' said Canton Colta's Roman Catholic priest, the Rev. Delfin Tenesaca, who is an Indian. 'Even the agrarian officials—I don't know whose side they are on.'

Already several thousand Indians from the valley have migrated to Quito, Guayaquil and other cities in search of subsistence.

'Even my brother went to the city,' said Sr. Lautibur, a 26-year old Indian who supports his wife and two children on a four-acre corn and vegetable patch. 'If I joined him, what work could I do? Maybe construction and roadbuilding. I would still be a peon.'[2]

The Ecuadorian Radio Schools for the Masses (E.R.P.E.) is located in Riobamba, near the Canton Colta valley, and about six hours from Quito by car. Riobamba is the capital of Chimborazo Province which includes over 1,000 square kilometers of almost uninhabitable land, some of which is at altitudes over 13,000 feet and covered with boulders and snow. Riobamba, the urban center of the province, is a quiet dignified town situated at an altitude over 9,000 feet above sea level.

In 1976, the Province of Chimborazo was in political turmoil. We had had nine years of an oppressive dictatorship; unemployment was at an all-time high, wages almost non-existent. Local leaders in Riobamba called for a general strike. The entire population responded. All communication to the outside was cut off and the functioning of the city came to an abrupt halt. The government sent in the military police, but they behaved with such brutality and their tactics were so repressive that the people went wild. Hunger is never civilized.

---

[2]Jonathan Kandell, "Land Reform Wanes in Latin America," *New York Times*, May 4, 1976.

Up to this point, women had not directly participated in the rebellion, but on the night of October 27th, a respected leader was killed and the number of wounded was mounting. I had gone to the radio station as was my custom to give my evening broadcast; we had to continue working since the *"Escuelas Radiofonicas"*[3] was the only local source of news about what was happening. Just as I was about to go on the air, the telephone rang. A woman's voice, distraught almost to the point of hysteria, came across the wire, " 'Senorita! For God's sake, do something! We women have gotten together in our neighborhood to try to find food and medical supplies to treat the wounded, but we can't do it alone! We need help! The situation is almost hopeless!"

This gave me the idea. I went on the air at approximately a quarter to nine the next morning and broadcast a call inviting all interested women to meet in front of the *"Escuelas Radiofonicas"* to ask the police to retire. By 11:00 A.M., there were 25,000 women in the street. They marched in an incredible demonstration! The government withdrew the police and, possibly for the first time, the people of Riobamba became aware of "woman power."

To be really meaningful, this event must be placed in the context of its total environment. The population of Chimborazo is incredibly poor. It has the highest rate of illiteracy of all the provinces in Ecuador. Well over half the population are women. A recent newspaper article stated that in Chimborazo, "one discovers an economic paralysis and social deterioration so dreadful that it is almost inconceivable..."[4] This is not new phenomena, nor is it just being discovered. We who live here have always known it was bad, but we have been unable to put it into perspective. After all, if one does not travel out of the region, what is there to compare it with?

The term we use in Spanish to describe this condition is *"marginalidad,"* generally meaning "at the edge of," "on the border," "not a part of the active whole." When applied to people, it refers to those who are unable to contribute to or participate actively in the society, socially, economically, or politically. *"Marginalidad,"* particularly applies to the rural poor, and in Chimborazo, this means over ninety-two percent of the population. A substantial portion of these are outside the "money economy": there is no "jingle" of silver in their pockets; they exist by bartering what they can produce. *"Marginalidad,"* as it applies to women is even more insidious: in addition to not participating in the society socially, economically, or politically, they do not even take part in family decision-making. The decisions which affect the very core of their existence are made by the men folk.

Paradoxically, in Ecuador, one does not find the profusion of statistical data and sociological studies about *"marginalidad"* that is available on other subjects. The number of research studies on the status of women and corresponding statistics are almost non-existent. While referred to occasionally in documents such as the National Census, under headings like "Mortality Rates at Childbirth" and "Indices of National Population," on the whole they are generally lumped together with the total inhabitants. It is impossible to tell what percentage of women are "econom-

---

[3] *Escuelas Radiofonicas Populares del Ecuador (E.R.P.E.)* or the "Ecuadorian Radio School for the Masses" (English translation) is registered as a private, non-profit, voluntary organization in Ecuador.

[4] Gilberto Mantilla, "Los Cercos de la Indigencia," *El Universo,* Quito, Ecuador.

ically active," and even when mentioned in this category, whether women are included who work in the fields alongside their husbands, but receive no pay. Since women are not treated separately in most studies, it is implied that they are integrated into the total data. In our male-oriented society, however, one wonders if this is actually true. Generally, such studies are carried out by men; only the heads of families are interviewed and these, also, are almost always men. And, unfortunately, in our society, most men take women for granted, but seldom into account. This is exemplified by an experience of "Escuelas Radiofonicas," through which the heads of the organization gained important wisdom and insight.

"Escuelas Radiofonicas" was founded in 1962 by Mons. Leonidas E. Proano, the Bishop of Riobamba. It was created to program and implement the educational aspects of his Integrated Development Plan for the rural population of Chimborazo. The Plan was based on the theories of L. J. Lebret,[5] the French priest; and inspired by the Colombian radio school, "Radio Sutatenza," which utilizes radio to disseminate a variety of basic training courses designed to respond to the needs of the illiterate and semi-literate masses.

After one year of operation, "Escuelas Radiofonicas" enlarged the scope of its program by adding a "Campesino" Clinic which offered several services for rural people, especially Indians. "Escuelas Radiofonicas," without explicitly intending to exclude women, initiated and carried out programs that were really designed for men, including literacy classes and the Clinic which offered first aid. Actually, there were no subjects offered that were specifically focused on women's needs or interests. As a result, our impact on rural women was negligible; they participated in the Clinic primarily as helpers, while those who took advantage of the literacy program constituted less than twenty percent. This situation continued, relatively unnoticed by the organization, until 1968.

Then, one evening at a staff meeting called to evaluate the achievements of "Escuelas Radiofonicas," including the "Campesino" Clinic, one of our regional coordinators stood up and said he and his wife had had a conversation he wanted to share with the rest of us. He stated that his wife was very unhappy and had complained, "You are never home! You are always somewhere taking a training course, while I have to attend to the children, the cooking, washing, care for the animals and work in the garden to keep food on the table!"

He had responded by saying, "But it's important that I know how to read and do arithmetic so I can help other men..."

Her reply was, "...and how about me? Why don't I need to know these things too? ...Only you men have your needs satisfied!...we women remain ignorant and forgotten!"

The husband was unable to escape a feeling of guilt because he had no answer to these tormented words. The plight of the coordinator forced the meeting to reexamine the entire program in the light of this new awareness. They were suddenly brought up sharply by the realization that, indeed, they had not given any particular thought or attention to the participation of women in the program: they had simply assumed that women would take part if they wanted to.

---

[5]L. J. Lebret, Dynamique Concrete du Developpement.

Having acknowledged this oversight, *"Escuelas Radiofonicas"* made a concerted effort to reorganize the Plan to include women and to consider women's needs. By 1969, we had developed a number of programs specifically for rural, as well as urban women.

For over ten years, I have broadcast daily, Mondays through Fridays, a one-hour radio program called, "Women's Issues."[6] It covers such varied topics as civic

education, first aid, political issues, child care, cooking, music, vegetable gardening and poetry. From time to time, I interview interesting people on the program, as well as sponsor round-table discussions presenting the viewpoints of political parties, journalists, educators and other professionals. I plan the broadcast so that each hour always includes five component parts: news, history, music and poetry, handicrafts, and miscellaneous. This last area is comprised of selected topics of interest and home management advice. I dedicate the music section to a different type each day: one day will be devoted to "rock" and other popular styles for young people; another day, everything will be classical; the next all Latin American; and so on. In other words, I try to appeal to women of all ages, both rural and urban, and to expose them to many styles and tastes. It is the same with poetry, except that I focus on the work of women poets.

---

[6] *"Temas Femeninos"* (Spanish title).

Our audience consists of the entire female population of Chimborazo which means about 155,000 or more.[7] We make a special effort to address the needs of the *"campesina"* because she represents the majority: she is both the *"mestiza"*[8] and the Indian. Because life in the rural areas is so poor, a high percentage of her number, especially young women, have come to Riobamba and the other towns looking for work. The only work she is hired to do is extremely humble and poorly paid. It is all she knows; she has no status, and she is still regarded as a rural woman. The fact that the greater number of *"campesinas"* have been severely handicapped by the inability to speak very little Spanish or none at all, has prompted us to focus a major effort in this direction. Since 1970, we have offered seven special bilingual workshops in Quichua/Spanish[9] on "what one ought to know about the home."[10] Literacy is integrated with the areas of home improvement, pattern-cutting and sewing, handicrafts, knitting, cooking, first-aid, and child care. All deal with the most basic information in accord with the elementary level of knowledge of the participants.

While the quantitative results of these workshops are not spectacular, the qualitative results are very exciting because they reflect a noticeable change in thought patterns and attitudes. Many of the women who attended, now cook foods which were previously unknown to them or that they had never tried before. We believe this is an indication that their family diets are improving. When we visit their homes, there are obvious changes that have taken place since the workshops. Some have separated the sleeping quarters of the parents from those of the boys and girls. Often the kitchen-living space has been partitioned from the beds. In addition, the animals and fowl are now being moved out of the house and sheltered apart from the family. These significant modifications are not the most important indications of change, however.

The most revolutionary differences we observe are those that relate to their attitudes about their children's futures. Almost all the *"campesinas"* of Chimborazo are illiterate until they reach adulthood; it is, therefore, normal for them to bring up their children the same way. Those who have attended the workshops are now seriously trying to send their daughters to school, as well as their sons. Many, particularly the youngest children, are successfully completing primary grades and beginning secondary studies. This is a giant step forward.

There is one unfortunate side effect, however. Many of the young *"campesinos"* (both boys and girls) try to hide their Indian background. They fear their classmates will not accept them or will make fun of them, so they adopt city clothes and customs which are not in accord with their upbringing. These urban ways create barriers between the young people and their old communities, and they gradually become strangers and cut ties with their families. It seems that this is part of the price that must be paid for progress.

---

[7] The 1974 National Census counted a total of 308,000 persons, 113,684 of whom were women over ten years of age.

[8] *"Mestiza"* literally means "mixed" in Spanish, but usually refers to persons of mixed racial heritage, the most common of which is Spanish with Indian.

[9] There is an on-going controversy over the spelling of *"Quichua."* The educated elite and academicians maintain it should be *"Quechua,"* while the humble people who speak the language continue to pronounce it as if it were spelled with an "i" rather than an "e."

[10] In Quichua, this is translated as *"Huasipi Ruranata Yachana,"* the name of the workshop program.

Luckily, this is not a general rule. There is also a strong movement among the young people ro preserve Indian cultural and artistic values. Many youth groups study indigenous music, dancing and poetry, and travel among the towns, making popular theatrical presentations designed to instill pride in our heritage. The more advanced educational centers are also contributing to the rescue of native cultural values through research and the teaching of Quichua, the language indigenous to Ecuador.

The effort of *"Escuelas Radiofonicas"* to place special attention on the needs of the *"campesina"* led us to closer observation of the *"Campesino"* Clinic. It became obvious that simply maintaining a "curative" or first-aid medical service was not a great contribution to the improvement of health. At the same time, it also became clear that if we wanted to improve health at the individual, family and community levels, the education and training of women was critical. We reoriented the Plan to include a health education program based on communicating with women. Professional social workers from our staff, in collaboration with government health services personnel, give ninety-day practical training courses to prepare young *"campesinas"* to become nurses' aides. The only prerequisite is that the young women must have completed their primary schooling. All the courses are supported and reinforced by supplementary radio programs on health. We also depend on the radio to inform rural women that the courses are available, as well as the services provided by the *"Campesino"* Clinic. For example, in my daily program, "Women's Issues," I try to give as much information as possible about common illnesses, particularly children's diseases. I explain about vaccination, the ages at which they should be given, and where they can be obtained.

Informative supplementary reading material is also available through *"Escuelas Radiofonicas' "*bilingual newspaper, *"Jatari,"* a small bi-monthly publication. The paper is addressed to a rural audience and therefore, avoids academic use of language. Nevertheless, because our objective is to improve vocabularies, we generally use the most proper or correct words and place the more commonly understood words, as well as synonyms, in parenthesis. We attempt to help the *"campesino"* understand the urban vocabulary so that when he or she goes to the city, he or she can understand and be understood, not isolated by language.

In 1977, we began incorporating women's needs into a "Tele-Education Program," a non-formal education/extension service designed especially to enable dropouts from, or those who had never participated in the formal educational system, to attain or complete their education. "Tele-Education" is predicated on the needs of adults in real-life situations and develops income-generating skills in *"campesinos"* based on knowledge which they have already acquired through everyday experience. In addition to academic courses which are open to all students, women are offered two income-producing areas of skills specialization: pattern-cutting and sewing, and health education. We plan to increase the number of skills for which we offer training, as the aspirations and interests of women increase, and to the extent our resources permit.

The Tele-Education system permits rural people to study at the time of day most convenient to their schedules, in their own homes or together in an agreed upon location in the neighborhood. It motivates self-education, but does not rely on books. The study program is led by field coordinators who are *"campesinos"* with special training. Each student progresses at his/her own rate, and works together with the collaboration and support of other students in the vicinity. This type of program is imperative if we are to reach that part of the rural population that is isolated, whether by geography or by their feelings of inadequacy.

Chimborazo covers an area of 7,014 square kilometers.[11] Ninety-five percent of the population of the province families lives by working the land—what there is of it that's workable. Of the 298,000 hectares of cultivated land, 460 individuals own 160,000, while the remaining hectares are distributed among 31,320. The average daily wage is forty cents (U.S.).[12] The annual per capita income is U.S. $68.76,[13] but for the rural sector, it drops to U.S. $40.00 because of the maldistribution of the source of production. Forty-five of every 100 persons is less than fourteen years old.

While *"Escuelas Radiofonicas"* has enjoyed considerable success in its social development programs for women, I often feel that the work accomplished is insignificant in terms of the enormity of the task. In Ecuador, the participation of women in cooperative unions is minimal: very few are affiliated with unions and almost none are on boards of directors. I am especially aware of the problem since I was one of the few when, as a union member, I worked as an instructor in cooperative union education. The main reason women are seldom involved in unions is because of our social traditions. In Latin American countries, the woman's position is always secondary; the action is left to the man. As long as this custom persists, as long as the woman continues to accept a role that only permits her to provide secretarial assistance, or attend to purely social duties rather than assuming more challenging responsibilities, the participation of women in cooperative unions will never improve. There are a few unions, however, where the number of women members is increasing, mainly because they relate to areas where the major part of the workers are female. Even in these areas, when it comes to electing the directors and officers in charge, the posts are usually occupied by men.

Legal assistance for women is another area sorely in need of attention. It is not uncommon for groups of young hoodlums to stalk girls at night, violate and rape them, and then abandon them. One such case received a great deal of publicity because it was one of the few to receive legal aid. A girl was walking home with her mother one evening when a car with five of these hoodlums came along, struck down the mother leaving her unconscious in the road, and kidnapped the daughter. When the mother revived, she was very near home and ran crying for help to the neighbors. The entire neighborhood mobilized and two of the men were apprehended. *"Escuelas Radiofonicas"* organized a radio campaign to help the girl and her mother who were poor and, as a result, two attorneys volunteered their services free of charge. The trial was very short and the men were convicted, but they appealed to the Supreme Court in Quito. The girl and her mother could, in no way afford to fight the case in the capital, and the men would have gone unpunished if the radio had not contacted a women's organization in Quito. The organization took over, found the necessary legal assistance, and the men were convicted. But this is only one case: the majority of girls like this are simply victims with little or no recourse to justice.

The government provides legal assistance for children through the Court for Minors,[14] a branch of the Social Welfare Ministry. The Ministry of Labor has in-

---

[11]One square kilometer = 0.386 square mile.

[12]One *"sucre"* = U.S. $.04. The *"sucre"* is the Ecuadorian monetary unit.

[13]National average is 3,500 *"sucres"* per year, or equivalent to U.S. $140.00.

[14]The Spanish name for the Court is *"Tribunal de Menores."*

spectors in each province to help laborers find legal aid if they are abused by their employers. But in Ecuador, there are no organized legal assistance programs for women who suffer at the hands of their spouses, employers and landlords, as a result of accidents by negligence and other injustices.

The country, as well as the province of Chimborazo, has a tremendous need for programs which recognize that it is the woman who ultimately determines the changes in our society's attitudes. The Ecuadorian woman must become aware that her status cannot improve until society regards all of its members as worthy of equal rights and respect, not because of their sex, but because they are human beings. This is not to say that different functions are not defined by sexual differences, but it is important to understand that a just and harmonious society can only be attained through respect for human dignity. Respect for rights has nothing to do with being male or female.

For those of us who work for and with poor rural women, the future is no longer dark and foreboding. On the contrary, the horizon is widening and our goals are becoming clearer, but there are still many uncertainties and obstacles to be dealt with. The problems will be more difficult to overcome if we women do not coordinate our programs with those of organizations that can offer us the human, technical and economic resources that we desperately need. All of us can and should play a role in this effort; we all have something to offer. A new way of thinking is beginning to take shape, worldwide; men and women must not continue to work in isolation. It is imperative that private and public organizations, alike, be willing to coordinate efforts and commit resources to accomplish the task of making woman an equal partner in the economic and social development of Latin America. This is the reality. This is the challenge.

THE CHOCO WOMAN:

AGENT FOR CHANGE

Marta Arango de Nimnicht (Colombia)

Before her interest came to rest on the problems of women, Marta Arango worked for many years as a teacher in Colombia, and with the poor. Contrary to tradition in her country, she gives credit for her achievements to not having married at an early age nor having had the burden of children before she knew what she wanted to do.

Her work as a teacher led to the study of School Administration and Organization for one year at the University of Pennsylvania in the United States under a grant from the U.S. Agency for International Development. The grant was extended for a second year, enabling her to continue her studies at the University of Wisconsin, where she received a Masters Degree in Curriculum Development and Teacher Preparation. Upon return to Colombia, she became involved in a research project related to education and social change of marginal groups. The need for curriculum reform and the fact that educational theory seemed not to produce very concrete results influenced Marta to seek better training tools to help people teach more pragmatically at the grassroots level. She again traveled to the United States, this time completely self-supporting, to earn a Ph.D. in Curriculum Development and Psycholinguistics from the University of California at Berkeley.

Marta and her husband, Dr. Glen Nimnicht, live in Sabaneta, a small village on the outskirts of Medellin, Colombia, less than a mile from where she was born and raised. She co-directs, with her husband, the Center for International Education and Human Development (CINDE) which has spawned PROMESA, a program that revolves around rural women in the Colombian region of Choco.

Marta's dream has been to establish an organization like CINDE that could nourish and develop practical ways of helping the poor to help themselves, especially women. She says, "The opportunity I was given to study in the United States opened my door on a new world; I believe similar opportunities are available to all women if only they were able to recognize them." Much of Marta's "you can do it" approach to life may stem from her father, a poor artist who struggled constantly to feed his ten children. When he concluded that landscapes and flowers would never produce enough money to do more than buy new pigments, he turned to painting religious subjects. Religious paintings were in much greater demand, and at the same time he was able to avoid compromising his artistic ideals.

Although she does not touch on the subject in her article, of perhaps equal importance to her work with the rural women of Choco has been Marta's impact on the Sisters of Santa Teresa who were initially responsible for attracting her to this region, where about 400 members of the Order live and work. In addition to nurturing Christianity, they operate the only fully-graded secondary school in the Choco, as well as most of its village primary schools; and maintain the only radio contact with areas outside the region. As a result of the Sisters' collaboration with Marta, they are incorporating courses in social development, health and nutrition into their curriculum for training future nuns, and she has persuaded them to convert their mother house into a training center. As a result, the Sisters will be able to enhance their learning about social development during vacations and retreats, instead of devoting the entire time to spiritual and religious exercises. Marta's influence has been instrumental in relaxing their eligibility requirements for novices to include *campesinas*[1] among those acceptable to the Order for religious training. This year they are receiving the first group of *campesinas* in their history—twenty rural girls from nearby communities.

At the request of the Sisters, she has also developed a special course for them on grassroots organizations which will involve the participation of local community leaders. The next phase of the plan is to train a selected group of the Sisters with the PROMESA teams to work in the villages.

There is no doubt that Marta Arango, herself, has become a powerful change agent.

---

[1]Rural women, usually from the poor working class.

THE CHOCO WOMAN: AGENT FOR CHANGE

by

Marta Arango de Nimnicht

The region of Choco is located on the Pacific coast of Colombia. Eighty percent of the population is black, seven percent is indigenous "Indian," and the remainder is a mixture. The Negros are descendants of the African slaves brought to Cartagena by the Spaniards in the early 1500's. All of the Indians belong to the Embera Tribe. They live at the heads of rivers or streams, communicate in their own language and subsist by hunting, fishing, and growing rice, *platano,*[2] and other crops. The Pacific coast is on the margin of life—socially and economically —with relation to the rest of the country. What does the future offer to Choco's women?

There are only three ways to escape from the region. There is plane service from Bahia Solano: three irregular weekly flights by DC3 to Medellin, Quibdo and Cali.

---

[2]A species of banana used for cooking.

The fare is about US$75.00 one way, more than some women see in a lifetime. There is the supply boat from Buenaventura. And lastly, there is death.

Of course, one can opt for the village of El Valle via the 18-kilometer road which links it to Bahia Solano when it is not washed out by the rains. Although the distance between the two communities is short, the trip takes an hour or longer due to consistently poor road conditions. Irregular transportation service is maintained by two "companies," each of which operates a rebuilt truck of hybrid ancestry converted to a passenger vehicle.

The principal means of transportation is boat or dugout canoe via the sea. The major maritime flow is to and from Buenaventura. Approximately every forty days, a supply boat arrives carrying needed products. When and where the boat will land and the prices of the goods it carries are the cause of much speculation. The gasoline it brings for consumption in Choco costs 20 *pesos*[3] a gallon in other parts of Colombia; in Bahia Solano it costs from 70 to 100 *pesos* per gallon.

There are mail and telegraph services in the villages of Bahia Solano, El Valle and Nuqui, and a single telephone line between Valle and Bahia Solano. Short-wave radio is the sole means of communicating with other areas of the country. The only short-wave sets in the area are at the police station in Bahia Solano and those that belong to the Sisters of Santa Teresa.

The region is rich in natural resources—good soil for growing crops, trees for wood, fish in abundance. The principal crops are rice, *platano, yuca*[4] and a few fruits. Of these, only rice has brought commercial profit because it is the most easily transported. Generally, the people cannot participate in the world market with their produce because transportation to the outside is so difficult and expensive. Commerce is in the hands of few middlemen, "foreigners"[5] to the region, who make whatever profit is to be gained from a financial transaction. The problems surrounding the export of rice also apply to the commercialization of fishing. Three or four businessmen in Bahia Solano control the marketing because they are the only ones who can provide refrigerated storage and easy access to ocean transportation. Thus, the average Choco family is forced to live at a subsistence level.

The basic diet the woman feeds her family is mostly composed of the readily available carbohydrates found in *platano,* rice and *yuca.* The only protein they eat comes from fish and an occasional piece of pork. Because there are very few cattle, the Chocoana seldom cooks beef. The scarcity of cows also means there is not much milk and, for the majority of the population, powdered milk is inaccessible. Nutritional deficiencies have had frightening impact on children from the ages of 1 to 8 years, but because mothers in the region breastfeed their infants up to one year, nutritional problems in the 0-1 year age group are less alarming.

The typical house in the region is made of wood with a thatched roof of palm leaves. It is built off the ground, supported by wooden, stilt-like poles to prevent

---

[3]Ratio of *pesos* to U.S. dollars is approximately P 40: $1.

[4]*Yuca* is often referred to in English as "manioc" or "cassava." Its root is a basic food in Latin America and is usually boiled or used in soups or stews.

[5]The people of Choco usually regard all outsiders to the region as "foreigners" even though they may be native Colombians.

flood-waters and heavy rains from entering. Nearly all the homes lack bathroom facilities of any kind, running water and electricity. The children suffer from endemic parasites, diarrhea and other intestinal diseases produced by the lack of sanitary facilities such as sewage systems and garbage disposal. At the beginning of this year (1980), for the first time, two villages began projects to bring running water to individual houses.

In sum, if one includes the extremely high incidence of malaria, the health level of the people of Choco is the lowest in Colombia. The situation is aggravated by the near absence of sanitation facilities and insufficient health services provided for the region by the government.

The illiteracy level is very high for the young people in the four communities of Choco where I am concentrating my work: the municipalities of Bahia Solano and Nuqui, and the incorporated towns of Valle and Pangui. Actually, there is a sufficient number of primary schools in these four communities, but it is difficult to carry on year-round sessions because the teachers continually come and leave. The climate is hot and wet, health conditions are uniformly poor; goods and services are hard to get. Bahia Solano perhaps offers a little more because it is the center of activity for the region.

Partial secondary education is provided by two schools in Bahia Solano and Nuqui, neither of which offer the senior grades, and by another fully-graded high school in Valle. This school, Santa Teresita Normal, run by the Sisters, is the only one in the entire Choco region where students can complete full secondary school course study. There is also an agricultural vocational school in Valle which offers four grades. The fact that there are not enough secondary schools to accommodate the areas' youth, obliges them to seek "better opportunities" in the interior[6] of the country. "Better opportunities" for young women mainly translate into working as domestic servants.

After three and a half years working with these four communities in Choco, it has been possible to develop a general idea of what an average girl from the region can look forward to unless things change. She can expect to have a little formal education—maybe even to finish elementary school—but she has only one chance out of five to begin secondary school, and one chance in twenty of finishing. She can anticipate having six or seven children who will have malaria and dysentery much of the time. Other family members may help with the chores and when they are required to leave the house to work, a grandmother, aunt or older sibling may be available to care for the children under six. At least a third of the time she will leave her babies alone.

She will get up around 5 A.M. and work all day in the fields, fishing, or making items for family use, hopefully, that she can sell for a few pennies. Her chances of earning more than U.S. $100 a month are about one in twenty, and the likelihood of belonging to a family with an income greater than U.S. $200 a month is one in a hundred. That is to say, she can never hope to have much money.

One of her strongest values is involved with bearing children. Since her earliest childhood she has looked forward to being a mother; in fact, she will be looked down upon by her family and neighbors if she has not had at least one child by the time she is 20. That she be married, or the kind of sexual relationship she has with a man, is relatively unimportant. It is not socially unacceptable in Choco to change men frequently—sometimes every year—and consequently a woman may have many fathers for her children.

---

[6]Such as Medellin, Cali, Bogota.

Caring for the children, however, is the responsibility of the woman. The man is free; there is neither legal nor social obligation for the father to play a responsible role. We are beginning to observe, however, that as the woman becomes better educated, her attitude toward the responsibility of the male is changing: community gossip over arguments and quarrels seem more and more to revolve around this issue. It is also interesting to note that in spite of frequent changing of mates, the structure of the indigenous family is closely-knit. During the tenure of their relationship, the man and woman do not tend to mix with other families. For example, I am aware that in some black communities a very cooperative spirit exists where the children of one family take care of those of a neighbor. In Choco, this seldom occurs. When the mother goes to work, she often leaves the children alone—even a newborn infant—locked up and without food.

The portrait of the contemporary Choco woman cannot be painted in glowing colors. In order to present a true picture of the Chocoana for this paper, we designed a special questionnaire which we administered to a group of 100 women who are participating in *PROMESA*,[7] the program I have been working for three and a half years to establish. This survey showed that the average educational level of the women was less than four years; only 5% had completed elementary school. All the women interviewed had children, averaging between six and seven each; 38% were married; 40% had a free association with one man; 7% were widows and 15% were single. All worked at home a good part of the time and at least two-thirds collected fruit, were engaged in fishing or growing rice. A few utilized locally-gathered fibers to make baskets and other functional handicrafts.

The following *Table I* summarizes the data gathered by the questionnaires on three groups of mothers according to their educational level: 1) those that did not finish elementary school (non-elementary); 2) those that completed elementary grades (elementary); and 3) those that had some secondary school training (some secondary school).

TABLE I
SUMMARY OF DATA ON WOMEN INVOLVED WITH PROMESA
ACCORDING TO LEVEL OF EDUCATION

	Non-Elementary	Elementary	Some Secondary School
Group average age	37	38	32
Average No. of children	6.9	7.2	4.1
Average monthly earning			
(*pesos*)[8]	657	950	3330
Marital status			
single	4%	30%	14%
married	30%	35%	71%
widowed	8%	4%	0%
free union	57%	30%	14%
Participation in attendance at			
meetings according to type			
religious	67%	50%	42%
Community	17%	21%	46%
parent	71%	63%	69%
PROMESA	79%	88%	100%

[7]PROMESA is the Spanish equivalent of "promise."

[8]cf. p. 79, para. 1.

A number of tentative conclusions can be drawn by looking at the Table:

1) A strong relationship exists between education and family income;

2) Women with more education are somewhat younger on the average than the other two groups;

3) Those with some secondary education tend to have fewer children, although this might be partially accounted for by their younger age;

4) Women with less education seem to have more informal relationships with men, i.e., the questionnaire indicated a higher percentage of formally married mothers went to high school (71%);

5) A greater percentage of women with more education (such as those involving community action, improvement of roads, etc.) attend civic meetings, while a higher number of women with less education attend religious and family-type meetings.

The correlations shown by the Table are similar to those found between the social and economic classes of many societies. PROMESA was founded as a promise to the women of Choco, a promise to give them the opportunity to improve their own lives regardless of social class and economic difference. Before these women can change their destiny, they must have an understanding of, and the ability to exert some control over the factors that eat away at them on a daily basis.

Although the future of Choco belongs to its children and young people, the mother is the first person who influences her children, by word and by example. It is she who makes the most lasting impact on their attitudes and personality patterns; creates their abilities to interact with others, to resolve or not resolve their problems. The mother can be an effective agent of social change. If, however, the mother spends all her waking hours working and at the end of the day is so tired she is ready to drop; or if she or her children become so ill or malnourished that they are apathetic; if she has no belief that tomorrow can be any different from today—nor the next year from this year—the case is lost.

We believe there are two factors that are fundamental to a woman becoming an agent of change: 1) she must see herself as a person of worth, of value; and 2) she must believe that she, as an individual, can do something to meet the problems posed by her environment. If the woman has a positive self-image and the will to act on her concerns, she will be able to mobilize others to help her. This concept forms the basis of PROMESA's philosophy.

A major objective of PROMESA is to improve the environment for the healthy development of the young children of Choco. This includes their physical health and safety as well as their psychological and intellectual development. In this way, we believe we can make a strong impact on future generations and at the same time, regardless of social class and economic differences, we can help present inhabitants to improve their lives. Consequently, PROMESA directs its efforts toward:

1. Improving the physical environment by developing understanding of and providing assistance for learning how to:
   a. Build latrines
   b. Dispose of garbage
   c. Obtain clean water
   d. Control malaria;

2. Assisting the development of health services through:

    a. Teaching first-aid in the neighborhoods
    b. Generating secondary services in the community
    c. Forming referral systems to hospitals and doctors in other communities;

3. Improving nutrition through:

    a. Information about diet and its effects on health and growth
    b. Introduction of new foods which can be grown in the region
    c. Demonstration plots for home garden projects
    d. Instruction and recipes for adapting new foods to local tastes;

4. Improving the psychological health of both children and adults;

5. Providing for and encouraging the intellectual development of children and adults.

Because we believe that woman is the most direct and effective channel through which these objectives can be implemented, PROMESA strives to:

1. Develop leadership ability and the intellectual skills of the women of Choco so they can work effectively with their own children and families;

2. Improve the women's feelings of being strong and able to control some of the variables that affect their lives, so that they can transmit these concepts and skills to their children as well as encourage their physical, social and intellectual growth;

3. Develop a clearer understanding of what is necessary to have a healthy environment and how it can be accomplished.

The process we use at PROMESA to achieve these objectives is simple in concept but more difficult to implement. It was developed by the organization my husband and I co-direct, the International Education and Human Development Center (CINDE), located in Sabaneta. In each of the four Choco communities, we began by organizing weekly meetings with groups of mothers of four to six-year old children.

At the meetings, each of which lasts about an hour and a half, the mothers learn a new idea they can use at home to help their children develop intellectual ability. For example, we encourage the use of more precise language such as saying, "The ball is under the table," rather than simply, "It is over there." They also learn to use specially designed toys and games that help the child to learn concepts usually taught at the pre-school level. We teach the mothers to use them in such a way that the children will discover the answers for themselves, and through this discovery, learn to solve problems and develop logical thinking.

These specially-designed toys and games are available for each mother to borrow from PROMESA's Circulating Toy Library. The purpose of the library is to provide toys and games for those families that are neither financially able to buy the materials nor have the energy to make them, although they are easily made with basic carpentry tools. This way, the mother borrows a toy and takes it home for a week with the promise to play with her child for 20 to 30 minutes each day. What usually occurs is that, in addition to playing with the child, she also passes on to the father what she has learned about the toy and what it can do. The following week, she returns the toy and participates in another meeting.

During the first half of the session, the participants talk about their experiences with the toys in the house, what the children learned, things of special interest about the toy, playing, and the interactions of the family. The latter part of the session is devoted to the demonstration of a new toy and activities oriented toward helping each woman improve her image of herself. The participants are encouraged to develop new games for the toys and to offer new ideas about their use, particularly as they apply to "opening the door" to communicating with other family members or the community. We discuss community facilities and their relation to a healthy environment with special focus on solutions to problems.

It became apparent early in the development of the program that it was one thing

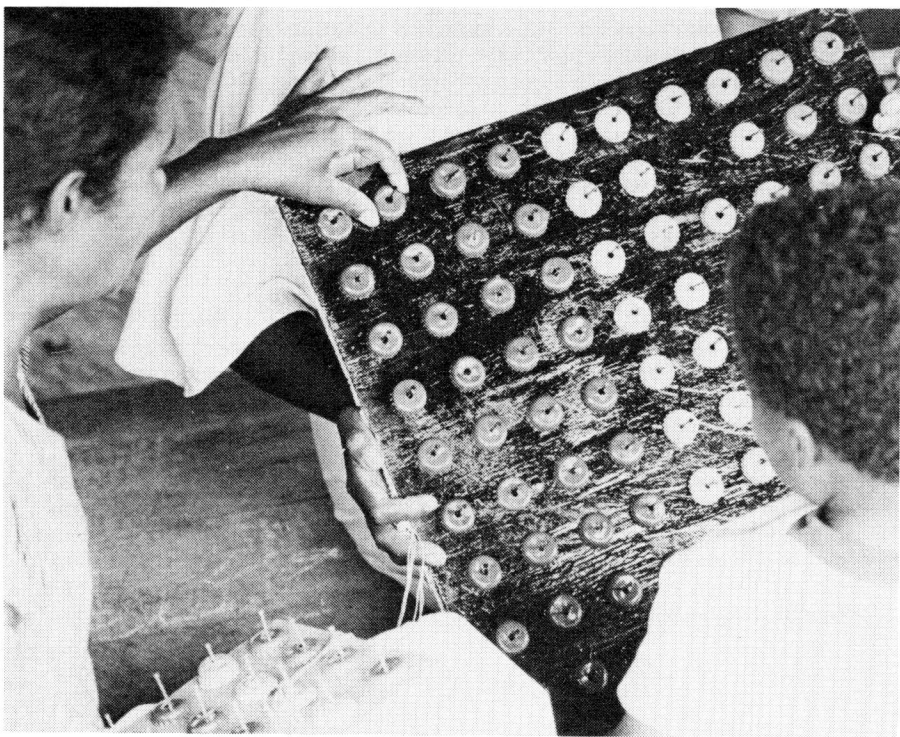

to work with groups of mothers in programs using toys and games, but quite a different problem to convince women to plant gardens to improve family nutrition, or dig ditches to drain water away from the houses. It was even more difficult to incorporate the idea of persuading the father or organizing the community to undertake a project. We found that making the woman aware of the small successes she was accomplishing by herself, such as those achieved with the children through the toys and games, gave her the courage to take on greater tasks, one step at a time. We discovered that the women develop many innovative ideas as they face new challenges with increasing self-confidence, but self-confidence is the key.

For example, some groups have begun using the toy library as a community center where both men and women can participate in discussing community problems. In one community where there was a serious problem caused by lack of drainage and where the streets had become mud-rutted breeding ponds for mosquitoes, the parents decided to raise money to buy several sets of tools to dig trenches to run off the stagnant waters. The tools were incorporated into a lending library like the toys, and are shared with the entire community. The project has been so successful that now they are purchasing a wider assortment of tools that also can be used for community carpentry projects. The toy and tool lending libraries are completely administered by community volunteers. Everyone pitches in to help.

All of PROMESA's efforts are linked to the belief that the woman is the most effective promoter of social change. For this reason, while the meetings of the mothers are a key link to the community, we maintain a parallel process in motion: the identification and training of potential community leaders who can take over the organizing and direction of the meetings, as well as assume responsibility for continuing the program. In Choco, I began the process with the part-time assistance of the CINDE staff which included a coordinator for training and the organization of health projects; another who works with evaluations; a consultant who helped with the creation of pamphlets and illustrative materials; and others on an as-needed basis. We believe the success of the leadership development is due to the "developer-consultant" role played by the CINDE staff, rather than the more conventional "teacher-leadership" method used by most groups involved in leadership training.

I am the only one of the CINDE staff who devotes full time to PROMESA. The past three and a half years have been difficult in that I have spent all my free time in training personnel, documenting what is happening, and deciding the kinds of materials needed and which must be prepared in order to provide the social workers[9] with the tools they need. We now have 16 community women teaching in the programs, and each of the four communities is organizing a PROMESA community advisory committee. The CINDE staff can now spend more time on the actual development of potential aids and solutions to community problems. We have devised several portable "kits" to assist the social workers, one of which is a mini-health kit that contains simple basic treatments for malaria, dysentery and first-aid. Others are a mini/micro-laboratory which we use to analyze problems of pregnant women; learning units for children of different ages; learning units for

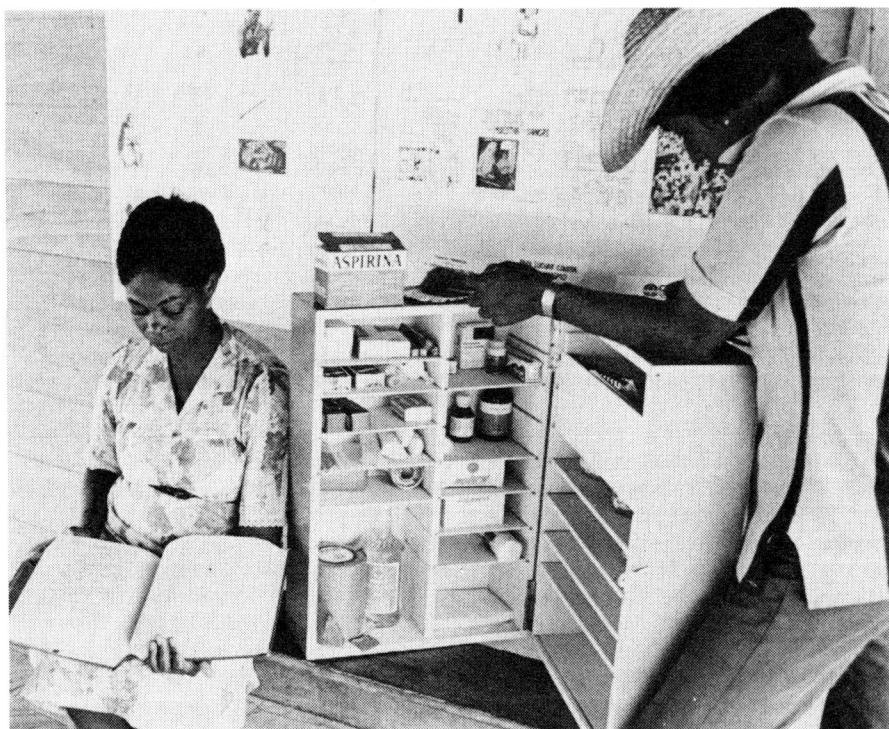

[9]The social workers are local volunteers trained by PROMESA.

blind children; and various other devices that provide solutions to problems. All are made of locally available scrap materials. Included are a small portable food-dryer, a simple water catchment, a compost-readiness detector and a hanging vegetable planter to avoid ground insects and soil erosion. With the assistance of the Center for Tropical Agriculture, we are progressing rapidly with an experimental vegetable garden in an effort to supplement the local diet.

Efforts to change traditional patterns of life and habits in remote areas like Choco necessarily take time. They cannot be rushed. Societies like these exist everywhere in the developing world. It has taken centuries to mold them, and the mold will not be broken in a couple of years. Organizations like ours cannot undertake such efforts without the financial assistance of agencies and foundations which are established to support development projects. Yet, we find ourselves battling on two fronts: the first, to change existing social and economic patterns; the second, to convince funding agencies that although slow, it is one of the few ways that positive social changes can be effected. To attempt such social change overnight would be self-defeating.

For me, it is very important to have clearly defined objectives, to know what I want to accomplish, and to keep my professional integrity in achieving these objectives. However, it is often difficult to maintain one's professional integrity and stick to one's objectives when one deals with funding agencies. We have no money from American funding sources and have found it very trying to communicate to them the kinds of things we are involved with. Some seem to think we are involved in too much educational research; others, that we are not doing enough community development work. We would like to find some way to better acquaint these agencies with the socio-political realities within which we work. It is difficult to believe that people whose business it is to be interested in social development can be so unaware of the problems; on the other hand, one cannot conclude they are disinterested, although it often seems that way.

At the same time, there are many European funding organizations who will give assistance to support models related to their pet social and political ideologies. We in the developing countries often allow ourselves to be led into developing and testing such models, even when they do not meet our own objectives. We have a few Colombian institutions that finance small projects such as ours, and while understanding the socio-political realities, they are usually completely unaware of the costs of such programs. As a result, the size of their grants are inconsistent with the objectives to be achieved. Most funding agencies seem to expect that their grants should accomplish far more than what is realistic within the time span allowed and the amount of money donated.

The money provided by foreign foundations to promote social development for women in Colombia has been very superficial. Many times such funds do not go to the projects for which they were intended, much less to women. Even when the money actually goes to a program intended to help women, it is seldom used for the most basic need, that of helping woman to improve her own self-image and concept of herself. Without this key change in her attitude, it is futile to expect that she can take advantage on a long-term basis of the other opportunities which may be offered. Although there are many small programs in Colombia which "do good" things for women, most are inconsequential if viewed on a long-term basis. In the poor rural and urban communities in this country, women must first be able to acquire sufficient energy—both on the economic, as well as psychological level—to improve their status, to move forward.

It is not intended that the program we are implementing in Bahia Solano, Nuqui, Valle and Pangui will change the opportunities available outside the region to the young Choco woman, but rather that she will be better able to cope with her own environment. She will probably continue arising at 5:00 A.M. with a long day of work ahead and it is not likely that she will have much more money in the forseeable future. On the other hand, her life will be more fulfilled and purposeful, and her children will be healthier and more comfortable; and most importantly, she will know that she can control or change many of the things that affect her life. She and her children can make Choco a region worth living in.

If this sounds a bit romantic, reflect a minute. If you can readily pick the fruit you need, easily catch the fish essential to your family's diet, grow a little rice and a few vegetables for your table...If you can help your child develop his intellectual ability to cope with his problems...If you can provide a sufficiently healthy environment to protect your family...If you can take pride in your own creativity and dignity...And...if you have the respect and admiration of your friends and neighbors, then perhaps those grand stories about life in the glamorous cities may not seem an invitation to leave what you already have. Upon closer analysis, you may decide you would rather not change places with someone who works indoors all day in a crowded factory—even if you can earn real money—if you must then spend that money to buy food that is very expensive and not so fresh at the corner grocery store. You may decide you prefer burying your garbage in a compost heap than having it stand and accumulate on your front doorstep drawing flies and cockroaches until a city employee comes along and carries it away—if there is anything left of it after the dogs, cats and rats have strewn it about. You may decide you prefer teaching your own children the values you want them to live by and how to cope with problems, rather than turn them over to some unknown persons all day while you work in the factory.

Perhaps we should give more thought to the redirection of education toward providing a more self-fulfilling life of the kind that is possible through the concepts of PROMESA, rather than the capital-oriented life on which high-income, more developed societies are based. Is it not possible that we need to redefine what is the "good life," and who are the "poor?"

In any event, woman must analyze who she is and how she wants to spend her life. The woman who establishes a more egalitarian relationship with the men around her has a healthy image of herself. She knows and accepts her strengths, as well as her weaknesses, and thus can control many of the conditions that affect her life. She can have impact on events, but not be manipulated by them. A feeling of "I can" pervades her life, and this positive attitude has great bearing on the way others respond to her, reinforcing her strengths and subtly improving her ability to act as a change agent. It is the reverse "I can't" attitude that too many women have toward themselves that keeps them in a dependent and inferior position, that never allows them to try to change because they believe it is futile. Through PROMESA, the Choco women "can" and are changing their lives.

IT ALL DEPENDS ON THE TEACHER

Francisca Ramirez (Honduras)

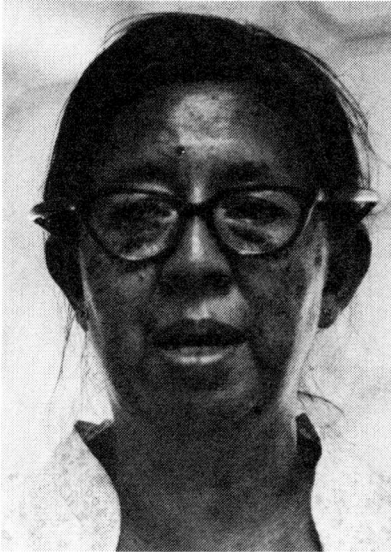

Francisca Ramirez was born in Tegucigalpa, the capital, of poor parents who lived near a Foursquare Gospel Mission and worked with North American missionaries. Her natural father died when she was very small, and her mother was left to raise her children alone. Francisca remembers that her mother kept the family alive by turning her house into a great kitchen, baking pastries, canning fruit and making peanutbutter, all of which she sold to the missionaries. At night, they went to church.

As a child, Francisca and her brother attended local public schools; later, however, her mother sent her to live with the missionaries so that she could get a better education. Although she remained in contact with her mother who continued to work for the mission, from that time on, she was raised by an American missionary family whom she still refers to as "Mommie" and "Poppie." On Sundays, they always went to have dinner at her mother's house.

When missionary families left their posts or went on vacations, Francisca's adopted parents would often substitute for them. It was during these times that she traveled and lived with them in different parts of the Republic which enabled her to learn about "campesino" life in the rural areas.

Since she can remember, Francisca had always wanted to be a nurse; as a child, her dolls had been her patients. Her adopted mother thought she should learn dressmaking, and wanted her to go to Costa Rica to study. Her own mother and grandmother sacrificed to save money from their meagre earnings for her schooling, and the Foursquare Gospel Mission assisted by arranging for her to enter the Bible Clinic High School in San Jose. In the end, Francisca had her way, and studied nursing for three years. Following the completion of her studies, she returned to Tegucigalpa as a nurse and worked for twenty-eight years at the San Felipe General Hospital.

Now in her late forties, Francisca is the mother of a son and daughter. For the past five years, she has worked as the head of the rural Health Center Program sponsored by the Evangelical Committee for Development and National Emergencies (CEDEN).[1] She personally founded the Health Center in the rural community of El Rancho, which served as the basis for much of her article.

---

[1]The "Comite Evangelico de Desarrollo y Emergencia Nacional."

IT ALL DEPENDS ON THE TEACHER
by
Francisca Ramirez

I am a nurse. I have chosen to work with rural communities at this lowest level, especially the women, because this is where approximately seventy-three percent of our population is located. My goal is to help as many as possible to improve their lives, to take at least one step up. I am able to relate to these poor rural women because I have spent the majority of my years with them; I am one of them. I have found it to be a great advantage in my work with rural health clinics because there are no communication barriers between us. We speak the same language; they are comfortable with me and I with them.

The truth is that I have not always been equally as comfortable with professional people as I now am able to be, because my family was very poor. As a child, I wanted to be a nurse and was always pretending to treat my dolls, giving them injections, taking their temperature. As I grew older, I knew I had to do something constructive with my life. I am sure that this feeling was probably because my parents worked for missionaries who became my ideals. I was only able to become a nurse because they gave me a helping hand at the right time.

Motivating the rural woman—making her aware that she is not making as much of her life or helping her children as much as she is capable of—is one of the important things which must be accomplished before any real progress can be made toward moving our country from the past into the future. Motivating the woman to do something about her situation, to use her potential, is impossible if those who might help her cannot communicate with this shy, withdrawn person who lacks education and fears all figures of authority. Gaining her confidence and trust is imperative; she has to know you are her true friend. And you must never betray that confidence.

Any successes I may have had in my work are directly due to the time I have spent and the close relationships I have developed with these poor rural families, building their confidence and trust in me, not as their nurse, but as their friend. The successful running of a rural health clinic is a very personal affair. It is imperative to convince the people who come to you that children should be loved, cared for, fed, given medicine when they are sick, and educated. You are privy to intimate family problems and expected to give advice on everything.

It is difficult to work with poor rural women with no education and very little knowledge of their own bodies. Building their confidence and trust is essential, but an approach that requires time and great patience. Little by little, their confidence in me must be reinforced by experience. When they can see that they have a healthier baby because they have more milk, and that they have more milk because they changed their eating habits at my suggestion—then they are willing to trust me to make other recommendations. It takes time to change their ways, to convince them to incorporate new ideas into their daily lives, especially when you consider that by doing so, they risk the criticism and ridicule of their families, friends and neighbors. Sometimes, the old ways are so imbedded in their customs, that it takes years to prove a point.

Motivation plus confidence and trust has been the only successful approach to ridding *"campesinas"* of old wives' tales and superstitions passed down to them from

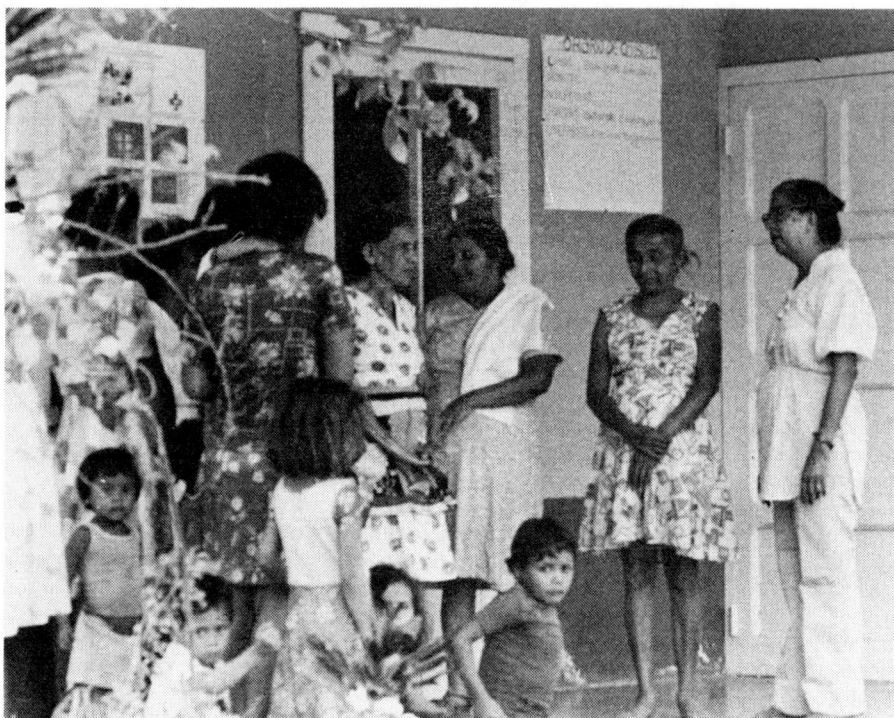

their parents and grandparents. Some of these ignorant beliefs are completely irrational and cause grave problems in their relationships with their children and other people, not to mention their eating habits, attitudes toward illnesses and family planning.

The poor *"campesina"* woman in Honduras is, without doubt, the longest-suffering element of our society. From earliest childhood, she has been forced to work. She has never had the chance to play with other children or to develop the ability to relate to other people through the kind of social contact that comes from school affairs and playground games. Almost since she was able to walk, she has been regarded by her parents as another pair of hands and feet. Because she is female, they also know she will not be able to bring in any money; therefore, she mainly represents another mouth to feed—something they don't really need. As a result, they have no hesitancy in requiring her to carry out the most menial and degrading chores, which in turn, places her in the lowest esteem of any family member. From the viewpoint of the family, she is something to be used, but not worth much in the way of attention or upkeep. She almost never gets to go to school, and even when this is possible, she seldom passes beyond the second or third grade.

The female of the very poor rural family generally passes her childhood doing small chores and insignificant work. She has not had an affectionate or close relationship with her parents because they have had to work during the day, and at night everyone goes to bed early because they are very tired and because there is no light. By the time she is an adolescent, she has retreated into herself.

Fear plays an important role in her life. She trembles in the presence of authority, which up to now has been represented by her father and other men such as the village priest. Given the degree of fear she has developed for her parents and others in authority, she has never dared to ask many questions. When she is approached, at adolescence, by a young man who suggests an intimate relationship, she doesn't know what to do. She doesn't know whether she should or shouldn't let him touch her; and whether it's good or bad. She is afraid to ask her parents and, more often than not, succumbs to his advances because she has been starved for the warmth of a human relationship.

The reaction of the parents to the maturing of the girl and her attraction for the village boys is interesting. Although they have never paid any attention to her before, the parents now start asking who she is going to marry and when. One can suspect than an underlying motive could be getting rid of that extra mouth to feed. In any event, there are very few girls who do not marry—the younger, the better—since she will be considered a family embarrassment if she remains single for long. Once she announces her intention to marry, her parents begin to recognize her as a person; their reputation in the community is saved, their dignity maintained.

Sometimes when no more than thirteen or fourteen years old, this young, timid woman transfers her fear of authority to her husband. His voice alone represents power and command over her life; she must not do anything to arouse his anger. She knows she is supposed to take care of the house, the cooking and the washing; she knows she will bear the children, as did her mother before her. Beyond this, she knows little else.

Her belly becomes filled with children year after year because of fear and ignorance. She is afraid to refuse her husband his pleasure, and she does not know that she has alternatives. If she is made aware that it is possible to plan her pregnancies, fear and ignorance again work against her. She may be confronted by a husband who is unwilling to use contraceptives and refuses to allow her to use them, or a priest who tells her she is committing a mortal sin. If she crosses the husband, she is afraid he will leave her or beat her; if she crosses the priest, she will be condemned to Hell. When women come to me with this dilemma, they want to change their situation but they are afraid.

My role is that of a moderator, and if I am a good communicator, a change agent, as well. I tell her, "It really isn't necessary to go against your husband—why don't you bring him to a meeting some time? I'd like to meet him."

If we are patient, she can usually persuade him to accompany her, and I listen to his objections, which may be rooted in superstitutions such as, "I don't believe in planning because the number of children you have is predestined." Political propaganda can be blamed for other objections like, "We have to increase the population if we want our country to be powerful," and, "Family planning is a capitalist ploy to keep the poor countries weak by reducing manpower." Others are based on simple economics: "I need children to support me in my old age." And then there is the simple reluctance to do anything which he construes as challenging his masculinity, such as "If she uses these things, what is to keep her from being unfaithful?" "If my children die I must be able to replace them," or, "If I don't have many children, my friends and relatives will think I am not a man." I also suspect that men subconsciously feel their authority is being challenged by programs that are directed at women, and family planning programs almost always are.

Initially, the objections of the men are reflected by the women in their attitudes and their reluctance to discuss the problem. I usually point out that the more children they have, the more they will see die. I show them how fewer children are easier to care for and that when the family is small, life for everyone improves. With patience, most objections can be overcome.

The women I am talking about are those at the very lowest level, socially, economically, and educationally. They are completely out of the mainstream. They make no contribution to society except the dubious one of producing children who, like themselves, probably will barely exist, but not much more. We must help

this kind of woman to become a useful person, not just a thing to be used like an animal. We must enable her to be productive by doing something to improve the quality of life for herself, her family and her community; not by producing one child after another to appease her husband's ego.

Although the need to motivate the "campesina" to do something constructive with her life is a special problem in Honduras, it is not unique to her alone. It is a problem shared by all our women. True, the degree to which we are prepared to do something useful is affected by our access to education, but education alone does not seem to be the answer. Those who are fortunate enough to receive an education, but who are not motivated to use it may be as unproductive as the woman who has no education at all. Both represent a great waste of our human resources. Both are also a great potential force.

How difficult it is to motivate people! If only the women who give parties and get their pictures in the papers for supporting the various orphanages, old folk's homes and other charities, would put their education to better use! In their way, they, too, are trying to accelerate the progress of their communities and our country, but they do only what tradition allows. They have not broken out of the past. Not that there's anything wrong with this; it's just that with their education they could do so many things that would have more lasting value such as helping people to help themselves. Unfortunately, the interests of most women revolve around their comfort in their own social world and at their own social level.

We usually base everything we do or believe on something we've already experienced, what our parents or our chuch taught us, or on what we perceive to be true in accord with our environment and the people around us. If Juan beats his wife, isn't it mostly because his father beat his mother and the children, and as a little boy, Juan perceived that this was the way men were supposed to behave? Similar-

ly, city women who have an education spend their time with clubs and associations where they can use their social graces and give parties because they perceive this is the lady-like thing to do. Their mothers, grandmothers and other women they admire did these things. Our society is less productive than it should be because we are handicapped by our cultural traditions that no longer serve us. Education is the best tool for changing ideas about superstitions and outworn status symbols, but much depends on the teacher.

Education can be an important element for social change in Honduras. Education, or lack of it, divides our nation. It is necessary to remember that all human beings can learn, and that social development is a process in which even the rich can participate. The woman who has an education and who lives in the city may not understand very much about the *"campesina"* or the effects of superstitions, poverty and fear on the life of the rural woman. She may find it hard to see any relationship between the plight of the ignorant *"campesina"* and her own situation, or believe that the poor rural woman has any potential for changing the economy, but the urban intellectual can learn, too. She need not waste her education. With her advantages, she can be of great value in helping the rural woman. Because of her friends and her education, a motivated urban woman who dedicates her efforts to changing conditions for her poor country "sister," can influence many people, including the government. She can open the eyes and ears of the powerful to our country's needs, where the problems are, and why. And she can *become* an educator.

The educator has the opportunity to become an agent of change. Because Honduras' population is predominantly rural, anyone who plays the role of teacher can either reinforce traditional attitudes, or open up new ways of looking at life. It can be a great challenge.

A good teacher learns from her students at the same time she is teaching; it is a reciprocal process that involves two-way communication. The basic elements are:

1) The communicator (the educator);

2) The message (the content of what the communicator is trying to get across);

3) The means of communication (instrument or method);

4) The receiver (the person or audience to whom the communicator directs the message); and

5) The effect of the message on the receiver.

The educator need not be a teacher in the formal education system. She might be a "promotora,"[2] an agricultural advisor, a crafts instructor, a nun, a volunteer worker of any kind, or a health nurse such as myself. The important thing is that she must communicate her message successfully, and the measure of that success is whether the message has the desired effect on the receiver. In order to achieve the desired effect, the communicator must really know and understand her audience, as well as her own field of technical expertise. Communication will revolve around technical knowledge because that is the basis of the message, but the essence of its success lies with the ability of the communicator to be tactful in adapting her technical knowledge and her sensitivity to the intangible human elements. Tactfulness and sensitivity are perhaps the most neglected areas with the majority of people who try to establish relations to "teach" "campesino" women.

A message makes an impact on the "campesina" only when there is some possibility that it relates to her needs and she can respond to it. It must be a message that moves her to discuss the information it contains; therefore, it is most effective when it is transmitted with emotion, empathy, feeling—with human warmth and understanding. This requires that the communicator be well-acquainted with the social structure of the specific rural area, the social customs, traditions, problems and interests. The most successful teacher is the one who learns from her students, her audience. She hears what they say, feels what they feel, understands what they suffer and senses the meaning of their silences. She adapts her learning to the technical knowledge she is attempting to get across, and in the process many new ideas occur. When she shares her learning with her students, they become motivated, and the process feeds on the stimulation that occurs. Each fuels the other.

In a rural society such as ours, we desperately need all our resources. We cannot afford to waste anything, least of all our women. The woman who is educated can share her learning; the woman who has special skills can teach them to others. The others can acquire the learning and special skills, and teach them to their daughters and neighbors. The key is a kind of social maturity: the willingness and ability to communicate and collaborate. But it all depends on the teacher.

---

[2]A "promotora" is one involved in "promoting" social change.

INTEGRATING WOMEN INTO RURAL COOPERATIVES: PLUSES and MINUSES

Bambi Eddy de Arellano (Bolivia)

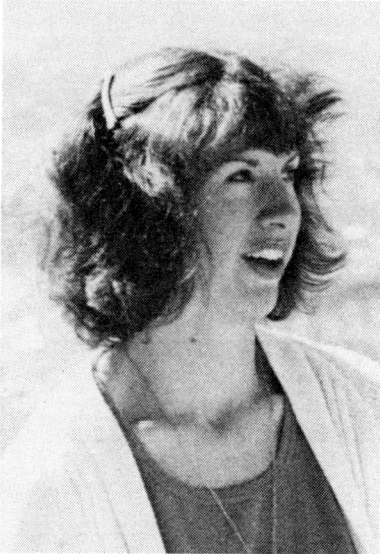

Born of parents who were Scotch-English on one side and Argentinian on the other, Bambi de Arellano is symbolic of a new generation emerging from immigrant families. Her maternal grandparents emigrated to the United States from Argentina when her mother was a child. Bambi grew up the third of four children, in an extended family living with her grandparents in the same house. She attended public schools and although raised in a bilingual environment, spoke only English until she went to Brazil while attending Cornell University. As a member of the Cornell-Brazil Project, she learned Portuguese en route to Rio de Janeiro to work with Brazilian students, and "picked up" Spanish when she later went to Mexico.

The pieces of her life began to fall in place when she became one of twenty worldwide applicants selected to participate in the Frontier-Internship Program sponsored by the World Council of Churches. The program was designed to bring Third World persons to the United States and United States people to Third World countries. By this time, Bambi had begun to immerse herself in everything Latin American. She had acquired a Masters Degree in Latin American Studies from the University of Texas and another in Education from Antioch College. She had been dramatically exposed to the problems of Third World women during her association with a bilingual program for welfare mothers in Connecticut, and was anxious to get back to Latin America. Encouraged by the professor who had led the Cornell-Brazil Program, Bambi applied for a Frontier Internship to study the issue of "Woman as a Person." The Internship took her to Mexico for a year with the Centro de Iniciatives para el Desarrollo en America Latina, (CIDAL) in Cuernavaca. There she met a Bolivian woman who had obtained a small grant to explore ways of enabling women to be included in development programs in more meaningful, less dependent ways. She invited Bambi to join her in a similar project in Bolivia. The World Council of Churches made the project possible with another small grant for two years and, in 1971, Bambi began her effort to persuade Bolivian groups, both private and public, to think through the causes and effects of the problems of the rural woman who migrates to the city. With Coordinacion de Estudios en el Extranjero y Asistencia Tecnica (CODEX),[2] a local private research and development organization, they co-sponsored a seminar in La Paz for all Bolivian institutions whose work in any way related to women, to analyze and discuss their objectives. Following the seminar, CODEX established an office to support social and economic development for women

[1]Center for Development Initiatives in Latin America.

[2]Coordination for Foreign Studies and Technical Assistance.

called the "Center for Women's Development,"[3] to train poor women and help them to initiate small projects in the urban *"barrios."*[4]

Two weeks before her 2-year grant expired, Bambi met Jorge Arellano, a young archeologist who had been working in the Andes. She returned to the States but after a short visit, a letter from Jorge convinced Bambi that her life belonged in Bolivia. They were married in 1974. After returning to Bolivia she taught educational psychology and sociology of education at the Catholic University in La Paz; worked as a consultant to the United States Agency for International Development to evaluate parts of its community development program that related to women; and became the advisor to the Division of Development for Rural Women, an agency of the Bolivian National Community Development Service.

Does she consider herself a Bolivian? She says:

In many ways, yes—in my commitment to my family, work in the country, working with the people, with friends, just feeling at home in this atmosphere—yes. But there are other things in terms of the training I received, the way I was brought up and educated, in solving problems and dealing with situations—these are areas where it becomes evident that I am not a Bolivian.

Bambi is the mother of two small sons whose births were spaced by another pregnancy that miscarried as a result of her work in the interior regions which requires extreme changes in altitudes, varying from 1500 feet above sea level to the 13,000 of La Paz, her home.

One cannot help being reminded of Bambi, herself, when she states, "My mother was never a *typical* anything." Bambi nursed her babies, manages her professional work on a daily basis, juggles her children between extended family, nursery school and home, and in-between has learned to understand "Aymara" and "Quechua,"[5] does her own cooking and maintains a 2-bedroom apartment without outside help.

Bambi presently heads a 3-year program called Appropriate Technologies for Rural Women, sponsored by the Organization of American States and the Inter-American Commission of Women. The program is focused on determining the relationship between the socio-economic role of women and the technologies they manage in three Andean countries: Bolivia, Ecuador and Peru. Based on the results, the second phase of the program will attempt to introduce small projects developed in terms of appropriate technology.

A generation later Bambi de Arellano is reversing the brain drain from Latin America.

---

[3] *"Centro de Promocion de la Mujer."*

[4] Poor neighborhoods and settlements on the edge of the city.

[5] *"Aymara"* and *"Quechua"* are indigenous languages spoken in the Andean region.

INTEGRATING WOMEN INTO RURAL COOPERATIVES: PLUSES AND MINUSES

by

Bambi Eddy de Arellano

Editor's note: *Bolivia is the fifth largest country in South America. The "altiplano," a series of large plateaus, the elevation of which is between 12,000 and 13,000 feet above sea level, is flanked by the Andes which rise to 23,000 feet. The region is generally treeless, barren, cold and windy, but supports approximately 70% of the population. The eastern Cordillera of the Andes chain connects the "altiplano" to the "valles," a complex belt of valleys that contains another 20% of the inhabitants. It is a fantastically convoluted region of jagged mountains that drops away into a myriad of canyons and valleys. Wider valleys sometimes offer a broad expanse of relatively flat fertile land. Crossing the eastern Cordillera at altitudes of 15,000 to 16,000 feet, the canyons and valleys descend into another main valley area which slips down from 10,000 to 2,000 feet above sea level, where the agriculture is practiced on steep hillsides. The sparsely covered steep mountainsides shed flash floods during the rainy season, while rising drafts from the summer heat bring destructive hailstorms that take an annual toll of crops and wash away the roads. Part of what is left for harvest may go unmarketed. Much of the lower valleys are accessible only on foot or horseback. An exception is the region known as the "yungas," a tropical area of deep canyons, year-round rivers, and lush vegetation. The "yungas" encompass an important agricultural zone which produces such semi-tropical crops as coffee, bananas, citrus fruit and coca (from which cocaine is derived). The low valleys of the "yungas" eventually give way to the "llanos del Oriente," an immense flat plain at about 300 to 1,500 feet of altitude, and containing about 70% of the total land area of Bolivia. It represents no more than about 15% of the population, however, and its commodities are small and widely separated. The flat terrain and great distances of the "Oriente," make air transport an ideal though expensive form of transportation. In the "valles," the terrain rules aircraft out, while on the "altiplano," it is more a matter of being financially out of range for small farm villages. The terrain in the "valle," is also inhospitable to railroads, so most traffic moves over the raw dirt roads that generally have been bulldozed out of the mountain-sides, subject to continual erosion and destruction.*

A railroad crosses the length of the "altiplano" but has little impact on most of the communities in this region, since it serves few cities, and is mainly an export carrier of mined minerals. Nevertheless, goods and people move, for most of the "altiplano" is level, dry and hard, and heavy-duty trucks can reach most communities without any road at all.

Pressured by international organizations, the Bolivian government has fostered the participation of rural women in socio-economic development through two principal types of programs: those that are exclusively directed at women and deal with their specific problems and interests; and those that are part of a larger effort directed toward broader national priorities and needs of small towns, neighborhoods and communities.

These programs were carried out by the organization with which I was associated, the Division of Development for Rural Women (DPMC),[6] an agency of the National Community Development Service (SNDC).[7] Often called "integrated community development," they were implemented on a national level by seventy-six *"campesina promotoras"*[8] who acted as extension agents and another forty-six who were "specialists" in promoting women's participation in social and economic development.

The significance of this effort is underscored by statistics which indicate that of the "Economically Active Population (PEA)"[9] in 1976, 61.1% worked in agricultural production. Of this total, 58% were male and 42% female. When one takes into account that these figures do not include rural women who work exclusively in cottage industries and small crafts, they tend to confirm the fact that the rural women carry out tasks which are fundamental to production.

In the beginning, the DPMC began its work with women's groups primarily in the area of "home improvement," i.e. the first type of program mentioned (related to a specific problem). After a short time during which a good deal of criticism was leveled against them for trying to isolate women, it was decided to look for ways to integrate the rural woman into on-going community development projects, especially those with some potential for a relationship to agricultural cooperatives. The strong institutional pressures which influenced this focus on the "integration of women"—the second type of program—also were responsible for initiating a new kind of attention to developing the grassroots. We began by seeking new ways to motivate rural women to participate in community action.

The established objective at the national level was to stimulate the socio-economic participation of the "campesina" through credit programs for agricultural cooperatives with development projects. At the same time, it was important that we create within the SNDC and the DPMC itself greater sensitivity and receptivity to active contribution by women at all levels. Both organizations are administered by men. Since this new emphasis on "integration" was a change in focus, information about it was distributed throughout the agencies and discussions were promoted at all levels. As a result of our effort, we hoped to avoid misunderstanding and opposition to this program calling for greater participation by women in the country's productive activity. Total acceptance within the agencies, however, was difficult to achieve.

One reason for this was that, generally speaking, there are two different ways in which people regard woman's role. The first is a kind of home economics view. For example, the agronomist will often look at the rural woman and see his wife—he will want to see her keeping the children clean, keeping the house clean, arranging flowers, putting curtains on the windows. And then, there is the other viewpoint that realizes that poor women's priorities are such that they just don't have time for such niceties, that they carry a tremendous burden in terms of providing income for the family, managing livestock and poultry, planting and harvesting. These two

---

[6] *"Division de la Promocion de la Mujer Campesina."*

[7] *"Servicio Nacional de Desarrollo de la Comunidad,"* (a Bolivian government agency).

[8] *"Campesina"* in Bolivia indicates a poor rural woman of Indian descent; a *"promotora"* is an extension agent whose work is usually with rural people.

[9] *"Instituto Nacional de Estadistica,"* **Censo Nacional de Poblacion y Vivienda,** Septiembre 1976, Bolivia.

115

very different opinions made it necessary for us to do a great deal of conscious-ness-raising among the technicians, attempting to get them to analyze why they felt the way they did, what it was that they visualized women doing. We tried to get them to think in terms of, "wouldn't it be good if" in the courses they held for rural men on water catchment, giving injections to cows, causes and treatments for animal and poultry diseases—wouldn't it be good if women could also learn these things? For the most part, in Bolivia, it is the women who care for the animals, herd the sheep, tend the chickens—they have a real need for such information. We found that if you asked women what they really needed, they would tell you, "how to keep the chickens from getting sick," or "water," or "sanitarios."[10] Many of the technicians simply closed their eyes and ears to this.

Within the DPMC, (as an agency of the SNDC, also expanding its activity to the national level), there was the need first to analyze what rural women's work in Bolivia actually included. Each DPMC "promotora" was asked to carry out an exhaustive analysis of her area and then to determine alternative ways that women might participate in projects related to agricultural cooperatives in the region. For example, in the "altiplano" of La Paz, where agricultural cooperatives had been long-established, were closed organizations and at the same time economically weak, it was decided that it would be impossible for individual women to gain admittance to cooperatives except through specific concrete projects such as small shops that dealt with items answering local consumer needs, vegetable gardens or raising chickens. These were seen as enabling women to acquire both capital and skills so that they might later be admitted as a means of strengthening the cooperative.

On the other hand, in the "valles" (valleys) of Cochabamba and Tarija, it was feasible to consider a more direct approach to introducing women for membership in cooperatives. This was because in these areas, women carry out indispensible roles in production and marketing, as well as the fact that many existing community organizations already had moved toward a degree of diversification.

By contrast, in the "yungas" (tropical zones) where the "campesina" traditionally does not participate in agricultural production, it was decided to continue home improvement activities. Emphasis would be placed on small income-generating projects as a means of seeking greater community participation. From this, one can see that the cooperative sector varies enormously in the three different regions.

Results of DPMC program varied due to a series of factors ranging from the response and support of the male technicians and the quality of the "promotoras," to the degree of openness of the rural men toward new activities for their women and the woman's own interest and motivation in light of her already overloaded responsibilities.

For example, in some areas the women considered that their limited available time would be put to better use in household chores and chose not to participate in projects. I have watched a woman's eyes light up when you present the idea of a project, and then seen the flame die when she realizes the amount of time it implies. When they tell you how much time they have available, they say reluctantly, "Well, we could meet with you every two weeks...or, once a month..." when you need a whole day once or twice a week. On the other hand, some of the small shops for local consumer items were so successful that the women were *invited* to join the

---

[10] "Sanitarios" generally refer to latrines, and/or bathrooms.

cooperatives. A deciding factor in the success or failure of this effort towards integration turned out to be the availability of the woman's time and her willingness to enter into new activities with a group outside the family circle.

While all the studies indicate that the rural woman in Bolivia plays a genuine role in the economy, and theoretically she should be integrated into agricultural cooperatives and included in agricultural credit programs, putting it into practice is quite another thing. As a national policy, it presented the DNPC with formidable problems.

Taking into account the constant challenges of this effort to integrate women into cooperatives, we tried to place special emphasis on training the field workers. One of the pluses of planning community development work in Bolivia is that we have a wealth of indigenous women that can be employed in promoting rural projects. As a result of exposure to prior training programs for agricultural and social workers given by various agencies over the years, women who speak the local languages[11] are available throughout rural areas all over the country. All DMPC *"promotoras"* were indigenous rural women. They were given community-level instruction in motivation, research, project planning, group organization and in transmitting their skills to others. The underlying idea was that if we could effect a change in the viewpoint of the *"promotoras"* who were all of rural extraction, then through them we could change the attitudes of the *"campesinas,"* themselves.

One of the strongest parts of the program was the relationship of the *"promotora"* to the community and her ability to communicate with the local women on their own level. She was with the community day in and day out. A first step in changing attitudes, we found, was getting the *"campesina"* to understand the causal relationships that affect her. It is often very difficult for her to believe there is "a way out," or that she can do anything about changing her life. The *"promotora,"* herself, may become an example of a *"campesina"* who changed her direction—a role model. But to do this, she must work with them, be in their homes, become a part of their lives. Their ability to meet with the women varied, partly because of the geography and partly because of the *"campesina"* time limitations, much of which depended on the agricultural calendar for planting and harvesting. May and June in the *"altiplano,"* for example, is impossible. Nevertheless, they tried to get together with the women four or five times a week.

In spite of the fact that the *"promotoras"* were relatively well-trained to cope with the problems of the communities and had the confidence and trust of the rural women, it was an uphill climb strewn with hidden obstacles to accomplish integration into the cooperatives.

The *"promotoras,"* themselves, were seldom included in the DMPC training courses for men field workers. Once in the field, the women were rarely called back to La Paz for training activities. Time and time again, we called attention of the administrators to this lack, to no avail. Some areas of training would have been greatly improved had there been mixed groups.

The financial structure of the cooperative often provided a roadblock to the integration of women. Cooperatives have always been considered intermediary agencies for working capital and the head of the family joins only with the intention of

---

[11]Many of the rural inhabitants of the Andean villages in the *"altiplano"* speak only Aymara or Quechua, ancient Andean languages.

acquiring a loan to invest in his small, family agricultural plot. On the other hand, over the years the fee required to join[12] had to be increased to cover the organization's expenses while their loan capital was rebuilding. In many cooperatives, the membership fee became so expensive—in some, as high as the equivalent of U.S. $400.00—that few small farmers could afford to join. One has to be aware that while the average income of the agriculturally-oriented family varies considerably, the majority are at a subsistence level. In addition, few women own land, usually only widows. In sum, the cooperatives' requirements for granting loans—land ownership and an ample amount of personal capital—was very discouraging, particularly to women.

After about two years managing credit which had been provided for their projects under a United States Agency for International Development (USAID) loan to the SNDC, they began to have a series of administrative difficulties. These were mostly due to the lack of management experience and understanding of financial administration. The problems revolved around farmers' delinquencies in meeting loan payments, lack of accounting systems, and inability to manage small units. As a result, USAID provided a new loan to the Bolivian government to restructure and refinance the program and advised the government that the SNDC and its component agencies should concentrate on building larger cooperatives that would include various services and areas of productive activities. It was reasoned that this kind of expansion would allow the cooperatives to increase membership capacity and at the same time enable them to improve administrative capabilities from within.

This modification of the program at the institutional level changed the work of the DPMC. Now instead of soliciting admittance of women to small agricultural cooperatives in each community, which comprised up to 40 members each, it became necessary to see that they join these multi-service cooperatives that would embrace from 1000 to 1200 agri-businesses. Insofar as the idea favored more effective work with rural women, as well as their integration, it was good. First, it offered a variety of services: credit for different crops, animal raising, small industries and crafts; agricultural and technical training; and consumer facilities such as marketing information and outlets. Secondly, in order to encourage new members, the share capital was reduced to something the woman might afford—she could buy in for around U.S. $10.00 if she thought it was worth her while. And lastly, because these larger cooperatives for the most part would be essentially new organizations, they would not include many of the more traditional and sometimes unfortunate viewpoints of the older cooperative movements. In Bolivia, these three factors could serve to counteract the principal barriers we had encountered in integrating rural women into small agricultural cooperatives. Unfortunately, the other side of the coin was that the larger multi-faceted cooperatives became replicas of the small cooperatives and magnified all their problems on a broader scale.

The first experiences with the larger multi-service cooperatives demonstrated that the obstacles to the entrance of women are not always at the institutional level, but

---

[12]Editor's note: Membership fee (Certificado de Aportaciones). The "certificate of shares" is an entrance fee or minimum deposit required for membership in the cooperative. It often can be in the form of a pledge to contribute a specified share to the cooperative in order to finance the operation of the organization. The organization of cooperatives varies from community to community and country to country. For general background information on cooperatives cf. Agriculture Credit Sector Policy Paper, World Bank, May 1975. For case studies cf. Tendler, Judith, Inter-Country Evaluation of Farmers' Organizations, Ecuador and Honduras, November 1976, AID/LADA, and Hurd, John et al., Cooperative Development in the Nicaraguan Context, AID/Nicaragua.

exist in the attitudes of the women, as well as men. It was observed that the integration of women seemed to have a greater relationship to her prior experience with community organizations, her husband's predisposition that she participate, and to the areas of production that the cooperative included, than to the elimination of institutional barriers.

Seventeen percent of the members of one of the large, multi-service cooperatives, Valle Alto of Cochabamba, were women—a figure significantly superior to that of most of the small organizations. Since the principal activity of this cooperative was dairying, an area in which the woman plays a major role, one might conclude that a greater motivation existed—on the part of the institution, as well as herself—for her to become a member. We found, however, that this is not necessarily true. For example, in the tropical region of Santa Cruz, another large multi-activity/service cooperative was formed, also with dairying as its primary interest. In spite of the fact that women also carried the main responsibilities for dairies in Santa Cruz, their membership in the cooperative never reached 5 percent.

Apparently, the difference lay in the cultural traditions of the two regions: in Cochabamba, wider social participation and mobility of women is traditional, whereas in Santa Cruz, the *"campesinos"* are colonizers who tend to live dispersed. Here, the woman's role is a domestic one which rarely permits her to extend her activities beyond the family farm.

Another unique example was the *"Pampas de Lequesana"* cooperative, a large multi-faceted organization in Potosi. It had no women members. This fact is partially explained by an idiosyncrasy in the economic development of this zone which has prospered enormously due to the production of potatoes which supply markets all over the country. Unfortunately, its economic development was not accompanied by any social change where the benefits of higher income were used to improve the conditions of family life. Thus the farmer, who as a member of this large cooperative may have participated in numerous loan programs and attained a substantive increase in his personal capital, would seldom use his income to attain greater well-being for his family. In this situation, the rural woman remains stalemated, while the man—beneficiary of the projects—learns to behave with more assurance at the organizational level and profits from its training and services. However, it has become a custom in the region for farmers to refinance previous debts with new loans which, in turn, caused a serious problem of sluggishness in loan repayments. The woman generally assumes a greater responsibility for obligations and debts because of the implications for the family. It has been concluded that if the cooperative had required the wife to co-sign the loan agreement as a borrower, the financial difficulties might have been resolved.

Overall, experience is showing that it is necessary to treat the participation of women separately for each cooperative, based on the kind of activities in which the women are involved, the potential benefits that attract them to join, the organizational capabilities of the cooperative and the degree of prior experience by the women in community affairs. Within the development agency—in this case, the DPMC—it should be stressed that all women field workers be equally prepared and in the same fashion as the male field workers. The *"promotora"* as well as the agency staff must be part of the field work at all times.

Recently, in addition to those stated above, a series of new difficulties for the DPMC has arisen regarding the USAID-inspired institutional focus on larger cooperatives. Technical and administrative concerns often make it difficult to insist that a cooperative project in its initial stage of development place importance on integrating women. At the same time, the cooperative is obliged to centralize activities of a large geographic region and its office may be distant from many rural communities. The distance alone discourages the active participation of the "campesina." Even when the community has its own group representatives to the cooperative, these are generally men because they always have had greater freedom and liberty to carry out business away from home.

Although the SNDC/DPMC/USAID objective was to increase the economic activities of the larger cooperatives and to assist them to significantly broaden their categories of production to allow new member participation, up to now this goal has not been achieved. They tend to remain tied to such general productive areas as milk, potatoes, or corn, thus discouraging the interest of farmers of other products. Under these circumstances, men can easily fill the credit needs of the family with their own membership, again a deterrent to women's participation. It is evident that until the cooperatives come forth with services and other productive categories in which the rural woman can also participate and play an equal role, neither she nor her husband will be able to see any advantage to both having cooperative membership.

In conclusion, let us attempt to summarize the pluses and minuses of the DPMC program, keeping in mind that the overall objective was to integrate rural women into agricultural cooperatives through on-going development projects. On the positive side, the potential for the program was great. The effort to incorporate women into a program of national scope can provide a forum for sensitizing those in charge at all levels to the importance of these actions. Such a global program offers the opportunity to broaden small project development training of the female staff to include cooperative development. The collaboration and assistance of the male technicians is a valuable first-hand resource when specific projects require technical knowledge that the women on the staff simply do not possess. A difficulty in implementing such a program, however, is that it requires careful planning and sustained implementation, not spontaneous or sporadic action—one of the pitfalls of past development programs in Bolivia.

I believe the program would have been more successful had we not been required to expand so rapidly on a national level. When USAID restructured its loan to the SNDC, it reduced funds to certain areas and increased assistance for a massive community development infrastructure which included schools, bridges and roads. The entire structure of the DPMC program changed as a result of the new loan. My own assignment also changed and I became advisor to the entire division for training and promotion, not for the women's program alone. We tried to maintain those aspects of the program that would allow the "promotoras" to continue working within the framework of women's special needs. It would have been better had we been able to focus on areas with an established socio-economic structure, rather than being forced to cope on a national level before we achieved any clearly positive results at the community level. While we were able to maintain a specific women's component, it became weaker. The fact that the objectives of the USAID loan called for concrete results, however, permitted an evaluation of its achievements and a reorientation of the program were it to become necessary.

It was observed that when multidisciplinary teams (comprising both male and female extension workers, agronomists and engineers) worked at the community level, they played a fundamental role in changing community attitudes, i.e. in convincing the rural communities of the importance of women's participation. The team approach was far more successful than when the female staff worked in isolation.

The principal problems encountered by the DMPC were related to the expansion of the program to the broad national level. Some of these were institutional; others were political. As the program began to expand, people came to the DPMC to inquire about jobs. Application forms were filled out and field personnel were selected by the regional heads for a variety of individual reasons, occasionally on a purely political basis. However, in the initial stages, most of the chiefs had a very clear idea of what was needed, particularly in terms of the technicians. The position of the grassroots supervisor that commanded a slightly higher salary created more difficulty than that of the *"promotor."* There was always an underlying argument as to whether the positions should be filled by persons with professional training,[13] or by capable *"campesinos."*

It finally became very clear that persons with professional backgrounds were not usually the best choice for this job. Their greater degree of education appeared not to have provided them with any genuine commitment to rural development or special human concern for the rural poor, factors which seemed to be essential to the overall success of the assignment. We learned that the best supervisors were the *"campesino promotores"* who had shown ability and had worked their way up the ladder, so to speak.

My belief is that when there is public knowledge that a specific sum of money has been appropriated for a designated project or program, a relative degree of political pressure of various kinds and from a multitude of sources will also be applied to the program simultaneously. Such pressures make it very difficult to insist that women be taken into account, particularly if the powers that be are looking for results in terms of their own specific interests. If these special interests do not include a sense of moral values and ethics, the persons manipulating the situations are "marching to a different beat." The results have a negative effect on genuine social and economic development.

One of the objectives which we were unable to completely accomplish was linked to attitudinal changes in men as well as women. As previously discussed, the acceptance of full socio-economic participation of rural women was not total, either at the community level or the institutional level. It will take a much longer time to convince the authorities, technicians and administrators of the advantages of greater feminine involvement. Even in projects which are exclusively feminine, a lack of autonomy exists. Perhaps the greatest difficulty in a project of this magnitude and with this emphasis on integration of women is the degree to which it depends on the willingness of the administrators to confront and respond to the real issues which concern rural women.

Those of us who have worked independently with "campesinas" are aware of the tremendous effort they are willing to expend to meet established objectives. But when work with community women represents only a part of the project, a great deal of this will is dissipated or lost. The degree of loss is a reflection of the predisposition of each local leader whose other work priorities influence, in an obscure way, the accomplishment of objectives specific to rural women.

Nevertheless, from my experience with the two types of projects—those exclusively with women, and those that integrate women into broader community projects—I have observed that in the long run, the *"campesina"* is more satisfied when

---

[13]In Latin America, "professional training" implies a degree of education, usually at or above the 6th grade level.

involved in the integrated effort. Even though the results may be more difficult to accomplish, it appears that the integrated project responds to her genuine need for participation and collaboration with men, at the same time incorporating the interest of the family and community. Rural women generally consider that the road to the integrated cooperative may be slower, but the changes implied are more lasting and have a greater impact on the community at large.

October 1979.

WHERE ARE OUR CAMPESINO BROTHERS?

LET THE MURDERERS ANSWER!

Myra Pasos de Rappaccioli (Nicaragua)

Myra Rappaccioli is an attractive young woman, blonde and fair-skinned, whose intelligence shines through her sparkling eyes. The youngest of five children, she was born in Managua, the capital, or parents descended from France and Panama, on her mother's side, and from many generations of Nicaraguans on the part of her father.

Although internally, the Pasos family was stable and traditional in the upbringing of its children, as far back as Myra can remember, her parents always opposed the dictatorship of the Somoza family. Her mother, a conventional housewife, and her father, an insurance salesman, were forced to keep their beliefs within the family, however, or endanger the lives of every member as well as their ability to earn a living. As with many in Nicaragua, their opposition was low-key because of their desire to protect their children and their elderly parents. Earning a living under these circumstances was very difficult; the family considered themselves poor, but middleclass because of their educational background. They were generous with what they had, clannish and protective.

Myra attended the primary and secondary grades at a school for girls run by Catholic sisters, the "Colegio Maria Auxiliadora." She was married before she was twenty to Emilio Rappaccioli, a young Nicaraguan engineer of Italian descent, and obtained a degree in sociology at the government-supported University of Central America (U.C.A.) in Managua. The Rappacciolis, Myra and Emilio, very early had four children and, like their parents before them, continued their opposition to the dictatorship. Although they were obliged to control their political feelings, Managua is a very small town, socially, and the power structure was well-aware of their anti-Somoza leanings. As a result, Myra was never able to get a paying job.

Myra's concern for her children and the injustices of Nicaraguan society impelled her to return to the university as soon as the last of her small children was in school. She combined her chores as a wife and mother of four with studying for a graduate degree in sociology, and there must have been many times when her professors wondered about the toast crumbs and marmelade stains on her term papers.

In early 1975, she began working with another young woman by the name of Paula Diebold de Cruz, (an American married to an Ecuadorian) on a research study of rural women. They, themselves, designed and implemented the study which covered six major areas: General Population Statistics and Laws; Human Resources; Health; Food Production, Agriculture and Land Use; Employment and Income; and Community Activities. The study, entitled, "The Role of Women in the Economic Development of Nicaragua," was published in the form of a seventy-four page paper by the U.S. Agency for International Development Mission to Nicaragua.

Following the publication of the document, Myra again sought work. The Nicaraguan Office for Women had just been established (1976) under the aegis of the Ministry of Labor. Myra, believing her recent study (the only one of its kind that had ever been done) and her experience would be of value, applied for a position. The study was given no attention, either by the Ministry, or the Women's Office which was headed and staffed by Somoza-approved women; and Myra was never considered for any position.

The experience acquired during the course of her research for the study deepened her concern over the plight of the country's women, and she began to actively fight against the injustices of the Somoza military regime—"the discrimination in employment, starvation wages, wife and child abandonment, illiteracy..." She joined the Sandinista Revolution in the belief that it was the only possible way that Nicaraguan women could recover the dignity of their sex.

Myra is presently Executive Vice President for Organization of the Nicaraguan National Development Bank in Managua.

WHERE ARE OUR CAMPESINO BROTHERS?
LET THE MURDERERS ANSWER!

by

Myra Pasos de Rappaccioli

Editor's note: *The struggle by the people of Nicaragua to free themselves from the dictatorship of President Anastasio Somoza took place over a period of two years. A major offensive by Sandinista revolutionaries in September of 1978, ended in an overwhelming military defeat of the rebel forces.*

A year later, in July of 1979, the Sandinista drive for freedom culminated in a resounding victory over the Somoza forces.

This commentary was written after the first campaign by a woman leader of Nicaragua's feminist movement who participated in both military actions.

The social and economic fabric of Nicaraguan society has been despotically controlled and manipulated for approximately fifty years by dictatorial generations of the Somoza family. Our men have, over the years, been cowed into submission by techniques of intimidation, such as black lists, no work, incarceration, beatings and murder. This debasement of Nicaraguan men has condemned the majority of our women to support their families at bare levels of subsistence by working up to twelve hours a day in "sweat shops," picking coffee beans, cotton, and cutting sugar cane without even the most basic human rights, let alone social benefits.

This tremendous struggle for survival obliged many of us to send our children at an early age into the streets to beg and steal, shine shoes, even prostitute themselves—anything so long as a few more pennies were added to the family income—so that the family could continue to simply exist. As mothers, we knew this meant the end of their innocence and any morality they may have gleaned in their few years, not to mention the termination of their skimpy education. Even so, these children were the lucky ones. At least they survived infancy. Parasites are endemic to Nicaragua, medical assistance for the poor unheard of. Malaria is a way of life and malnutrition is the expected norm. These, and many other deprivations claim the lives of most of our children before they reach their first birthday.

Because of the poverty wages and inadequate income level even when work can be found, countless families have been forced to make their homes in hovels comprised basically of carefully split cardboard boxes, reinforced with tin cans that have been cut lengthwise and pounded flat, or whatever other scraps that are available. These materials are shaped around beams of rotten wood that are found discarded in piles of rubbish, then secured with hemp and rusty, bent nails that the children straighten. These shacks are called home, and have no running water or sanitary facilities of any kind. The one central source of fresh water in some neighborhoods is also used as the communal garbage dump and cesspool. Cases of typhus, typhoid fever, and cholera are common. The floors in many homes are composed of packed earth with fleas and lice continually present. Their bites aren't so bad, but sometimes they bring terrible diseases.

In the event of catastrophes such as earthquakes and epidemics, there are virtually no medical facilities available for the poor. An epidemic is like a huge forest fire raging out of control. Eventually it will burn itself out. The difference is that one burns trees to death; in Nicaragua, it kills people. The government of Nicaragua under the leadership of the Somozas has not believed it necessary to provide medical considerations for the poor. Those with little or no income have had to rely on the meagre, but appreciated, help of the Church, the International Red Cross and a few others, for assistance.

The Somozan regime has obliterated all rights of the people of Nicaragua to such extremes that we have been forced to turn en masse to the Somoza-controlled Liberal Party for our survival. By doing so, we are allowed to earn just enough so that we will not perish. Membership in the Party is a principal requirement before one can apply for any job paid by the government. Membership of the citizenry has guaranteed Somoza complete control. Somoza-sponsored surveys indicate that it is the will of the electorate that we have no upgrading of Nicaraguan society, especially as it would affect upward mobility of the "campesinos" and any alleviation of their miserable plight.

Between 1974 and 1976, the peoples' constitutional rights were totally abridged. Martial law was imposed and a cloud of censorship engulfed our communications system. These suppressive measures were instituted by the dictatorship so that hideous crimes could be disguised and concealed from the citizens of Nicaragua, as well as the world at large.

Plunder of public funds has been a way of life in Nicaragua from the time the Somozas took over, but the last few years also have been marked by a tremendous upsurge in the embezzlement of national funds by government officials. Military tribunals preside over civil cases, the outcomes of which invariably lead to complete deprivation of all constitutional guarantees. At first, wholesale imprisonment and torture were the methods used to quiet disorder among the disenfranchized masses. Gradually, the harshness of the punitive measures escalated into wanton murder of men, women and even children suspected of any crime or disloyalty to the state.

In the context of this social and political repression, a group of 60 concerned women (who as of this writing, prefer to remain anonymous because of possible future retribution) banded together on September 29, 1977, and organized the Association of Women in the Presence of National Problems (AMPRONAC).[1] One of their purposes was to focus attention on the inequities caused by the Somozan regime.

Later on in 1977, we had a meeting to work on the possible ways of organizing our association in such a manner that we could involve ourselves at all levels in the political and social action of the country. We determined that our objectives were clear. We drastically needed women of all social and economic levels to participate in the research and solution of the overwhelming problems raised by the national crisis brought on by Somozan oppression. In order to immediately begin the work of exposing the crimes committed by the government, we created a fund-raising committee to finance the organization. We also decided that the social, political and economic rights of women in particular, as well as those of the general population of Nicaragua must be regained at any cost. It was clear that AMPRONAC was an association comprised of women who were highly motivated by their ideals to create a nation free of oppression and despotic tyranny.

At the end of 1977, the censorship restrictions were lifted. Gradually, opposition to the regime intensified as people were able to meet to discuss their grievances in

---

[1] Asociacion de la Mujer Ante la Problematica Nacional.

churches and the universities. One such meeting held in November 1977, attracted over a thousand people and developed a slogan, **"Where are our 'campesino' brothers?"** to attract others into the popular movement. Later, students added, **"Let the murderers answer!"** to the slogan in a direct reference to Somoza's moral insensibilities.

By late November, AMPRONAC had joined with other organizations in a united coalition to demonstrate against Somoza by a massive protest march in Managua. Before we were able to take to the street, however, police cadres invaded AMPRONAC headquarters, as well as other major meeting places, and effectively destroyed our coordinated efforts. The demonstration fell apart. The police enforced their authority with planes and helicopters, machine-gunning many who resisted. Others were imprisoned; some never to be seen again. The movement was quelled for a short time.

In January, however, three events took place which erased the reticence that had restrained many people and detonated the dormant time bomb of hatred by the people for all the wrongs heaped on them by the dictatorship. The first was the murder of Pedro Joaquin Chamorro, publisher and editor of a prominent newspaper and a well-known opponent of Somoza. In response, the vast majority of the population united in a national labor strike which effectively brought all government functions to a halt. A short time later, relatives of people who had mysteriously disappeared and political prisoners still held captive, took control of the United Nations headquarters in Managua. A hundred thousand sympathizers erupted in a massive demonstration carrying placards and shouting, **"Punish the assassins of Pedro Joaquin Chamorro!"** They condemned the policies of the Somoza regime which spanned a period over more than forty years. Their hate was evident. AMPRONAC took great pride in joining our sisters and brothers in the rebellion which lasted for two weeks. Later, on January 30th, we of AMPRONAC organized a demonstration consisting of more than six hundred women from all levels of society in a peaceful march protesting our social grievances. Within three hours the National Guard dissolved our demonstration. Under the personal leadership of Somoza's son, "Tacho" Somoza III, and Chief of Police, Alisio Gutierrez, riot squads freely dispensed tear-gas and physical brutality to disperse the unarmed women. We had been prepared for tear-gas—all of us carried handkerchiefs soaked in lemonade and bicarbonate—but none of us was prepared for the verbal abuse and rifle butts that rained upon us with equal vigor.

AMPRONAC learned a valuable lesson from this experience. We carried out an evaluation of the January demonstrations, as well as our role in them. We concluded that the mass movement to overthrow the regime had failed because of the lack of organization and coordination. Our own contributions to the effort, consisting of denunciations and supportive resources, had had little effect. It was clear that if we expected to play a role in the decisions which would affect our country's political future, AMPRONAC would have to concentrate on organizing women and converting them into a force for mass action.

Our political focus moved from one of passive demonstration to radical action. Our goals were no longer vague and idealistic; we were able to define them precisely as:

—Termination of harrassment and repression
—Freedom to organize
—Liberty for all political prisoners
—Punishment for those guilty of barbaric crimes against the people

—Abolishment of all discriminatory laws against women
—Equal wages for equal work
—Termination of the exploitation and commercialization of women

To make the masses aware of our platform, AMPRONAC initiated Nicaraguan Women's Week, a celebration commemorating our fight to free ourselves from oppression. It was our desire to have all women participating in the struggle—not only for their own freedom and their inherent rights as human beings, but for the country as a whole. In so doing, our country, and particularly women, would shed themselves of the constraints of the centuries-old bias which impeded the progress of our nation in the contemporary world.

The effort to rid our country of Somoza became more intense during February, March and April of 1978. Women from every walk of life, every town and city, had become involved. We began fighting harder than ever before. As our ardor increased, we all became aware of radical changes taking place within ourselves as women. Day by day, we were becoming more militant in nature and more strident in our demands. Although it had begun in the streets with political rebellion, it eventually encompassed every facet of our lives. The slogans became a part of us and affected our relationships at home and at work. Our husbands, especially, were drastically affected by the change overcoming their once docile, obedient wives. No longer were women willing to be put down and treated as inferiors, catering to their every demand. We were at least their equals and every day we became more and more aware of that fact. If we were equal to our men in battle, to bleed and die for our mutual cause, then we considered ourselves equal in all other aspects of shared responsibility.

During these months, AMPRONAC continued to organize demonstrations, with increasing numbers of women participating. We conducted a sit-in at various government offices and at the Red Cross dispensaries to gain "The liberty of Maria del Carmen Gomez de Palma." Maria Gomez was a young woman, who had been imprisoned by government troops earlier in the year and now was in her ninth month of pregnancy. She embodied the spirit of our women's movement and placards were displayed everywhere emblazoned with the statement: **"Every mother has the right to raise her child in liberty!"**

In early April, we instigated a hunger strike promoting the Field Workers Union. Its aim was to call the attention of Somoza to the hunger and despicable working conditions of the *"campesinos"* in the surrounding rural areas.

Government reaction to these demonstrations was predictable. The police descended on us in droves, murdering and maiming the people taking part. Because of our contribution, the stature of AMPRONAC grew in the eyes of Nicaraguans everywhere. We were ready to stake everything on the cause which was worth more than our lives. The dynamics of this image, our fighting and dying for peoples' rights, unleashed the meek from their burdens of fear. Massive numbers of women and men came forward to join in our movement. The conscience of our people was awakening to the spirit of rebellion against the forces of tyranny.

During this time of mobilizing the general population, the women of AMPRONAC began to drift apart. A gradual polarization of political beliefs and attitudes, diametrically in opposition, took shape. The basis for the split was the fundamental social composition of our organization.

Some of AMPRONAC's original founders were well-meaning, mainly upper-class women who had wanted to do something to help the poor of Nicaragua, but whose sense of social obligation was overshadowed by a well-developed class consciousness. They lacked any genuine desire to help the oppressed for a number of reasons. It was safer, easier and more comfortable to maintain the pretense of helping to alleviate the plight of the poor. It gave them something to talk about at their meetings, over tea and cake. They could feel proud of themselves for offering their help, although it was more fun to talk about than to actually act upon. It also met with the approval of the First Lady and her social secretary, which improved their social status. These women considered themselves moderate in their political outlook. ·

Somewhat later, younger women of varying backgrounds, who fervently believed in our format of aid for the poor and disenfranchised, joined the organization. These aggressive, educated and liberal women were also highly aware of the developing consciousness of world-wide womanhood. They greatly desired to incorporate progressive attitudes concerning women into the basics of AMPRONAC's organization. This attitude of social liberation met with disapproval by the ladies of the Somozan establishment who were the moderates of the group.

This division within the organization needed to be clarified and resolved; otherwise, dissolution was inevitable. We, therefore, set up a seminar to discuss our problems, as well as give direction to ways by which a united AMPRONAC could help solve the growing national crisis.

The seminar lasted until May, pivoting about the two factions and the disparity between them. The progressive forces pressed for radical solutions and treatment of the national crisis as one of a structural nature. They contended that the only alternative to the present set of circumstances was the complete dismantling of the repressive government of Somoza's military dictatorship, and a sweeping reformation. To take its place, they wanted to create a national government with representative participation by all the forces that fought against the regime. This solution was called "The Popular Alternative."

The reactionary members of AMPRONAC advocated a solution by which the dictatorship would be maintained, with only minimal changes to the social and economic structure of the country, maintaining Somozism without Somoza. This alternative was termed "The Middle-Class Alternative."

The seminar produced tremendous friction within the organization and eventually resulted in many members resigning. Those of us that remained, however, were bound together by a concensus of opinion in a united front. "The Popular Alternative" was favored as the means by which our cause could best be served.

The summer of 1978 saw a continuation of the confrontations between the National Guard and demonstrators. Violence was the predominant characteristic of the Somozan military forces, and they murdered all who opposed them. In Jinotepe, a small city close to Managua, sixteen young men were executed by the National Guard without trial. They purportedly had committed crimes against the government, but there was no evidence whatsoever. Later, the bodies were dumped in front of their homes with red and black-colored handkerchiefs tied around their necks, a government allusion to the dead men's sympathy for the Sandinista guerrillas. ·

In Jinotepe, as in many other towns, the churches were machine-gunned, and even very young people were hunted down and brutally killed. Nevertheless, our heroic people fought on tenaciously. We learned how to blitz the BECATS (Somoza's "Special Brigades Against Terrorist Attacks") with home-made bombs. Molotov cocktails were used to blast tanks and burn the houses of informers. The fight was very lopsided in favor of the regime, but in spite of the odds, we were uncompromising and resolute in spirit.

In August, Somoza issued a new decree which demanded additional taxes to pay for new armaments for his troops. Citizens of Nicaragua were not about to pay for weapons to be used against them. Even Somoza's own Department of Commerce refused to acknowledge the new law. Again, a general strike swept the country in protest. The revolutionary forces declared they would continue indefinitely, until the law was rescinded. We could not be sure, however, that all the people were ready for the consequences of such a strike. Considering the possibility of greater repression by Somoza and taking into account our lack of arms, we started planning for a wave of new harassments, such as house to house searches by the National Guard for those suspected of crimes. To this end, we utilized ghetto tactics. We secured our communications system through the use of runners, arranged hidden rooms in basements to take care of the wounded, and prepared predesignated escape routes for those in need. We organized ourselves by neighborhoods, and then by blocks.

At long last, on September 9th, the FSLN (Sandinista National Liberation Front) responded to the decades of tyranny in an armed offensive comprising thousands of volunteers. Throughout the nation, National Guard stations were attacked and destroyed, with our women fighting and dying side by side with the men.

The government retaliated brutally. The Air Force bombed cities and towns into rubble. Hundreds were executed, thousands more were jailed and tortured. The regime ordered a state of siege and martial law was invoked.

The rebellion was short-lived. The government had secured, in a matter of days, a complete military victory over the people. Nevertheless, they were not victorious over our spirit and desire for freedom.

We have yet a long way to go, but the will of the Nicaraguan people will eventually triumph. We know this now. And when we are victorious in exorcising the cancer of the Somoza family, it will be a victory of the masses. It is important to point out that the full active participation of Nicaraguan women in the Revolution has been and will continue to be imperative. We comprise 50.2 percent of the total population, so it is obvious that a *peoples'* rebellion cannot occur with only part of the people participating.

AMPRONAC is aware that it does not always satisfy or meet with the approval of the great international feminist movements. The rhetoric of our celebration of Nicaraguan Women's Week, as well as our general objectives, have always placed major emphasis on the struggle of our people for a free country. What other feminist movements do not always understand is that our objectives respond to the cry of the *common* Nicaraguan woman—the woman of the masses who wants an equal role in constructing a new Nicaragua. For this, we are willing to fight and die alongside our men. We are willing to bear an equal share of the burden, but we also demand equal rights.

People of the world, the women of AMPRONAC and the people of Nicaragua are grateful for your aid in our fight to free ourselves from Somozan domination. Your continued support in the future will be indispensable to our victory.

SOME SOW, OTHERS REAP

Maria Esperanza Briceno (Colombia)

Maria Esperanza Briceno was born in the State of Santander, the seventh of the nine children of Juan Francisco Briceno and his wife, Teresa Jauregui de Briceno. Her mother was from Santander del Norte on the Venezuelan border; her father, a cattleman, was a Venezuelan landowner who expanded his holdings into the pasturelands of the Northeastern Cordillera of Colombia. Initially, the family lived in Cucuta where the surrounding territory is so rugged that it was easier to maintain communication toward Venezuela than the adjacent part of Colombia. Family business interests prospered and they lived comfortably on one of their ranches until Juan Francisco's death when Maria Esperanza was six years old. Her mother was left with four young daughters and five sons, the youngest of whom was only five months old. She found herself with huge debts she had no knowledge of, and papers deeding all the family's property to someone else. Life for Teresa de Briceno and her nine children changed overnight: suddenly, they had nothing but each other and a few personal belongings.

One of Maria Esperanza's mother's strongest values was education. Her greatest concern was that her children not have to forego their schooling. Little by little, she sold all her personal belongings of any value so that the children could go to boarding schools. "As soon as each of us finished his or her education and could go to work, the major part of the money we earned went to helping Mama and to pay for the schooling of the younger ones." Of all the people she has known, Maria Esperanza readily admits it has been her mother who had the greatest influence on her life. "With all her problems, she was never bitter," Maria Esperanza says, "nor did she ever allow us to feel sorry for ourselves."

The children were boarding students at the School of the Sisters of the Presentation, in Bogota, from kindergarten through the fifth grade. At the time, the widow lived in Chinaco and it took three days for the children to get to Bogota by bus. "It left at 2 o'clock in the morning, and stopped at every village to deliver mail along the way. The mountain roads were treacherous and twisting, and as I look back, extremely dangerous. Yet, twice a year we made that trip," Maria Esperanza says. There was not enough money for them to go home for vacations, so they stayed at the school from February through November, all through the holidays including Easter.

From the sixth grade through secondary school, Maria Esperanza studied at the school of the Dominican Sisters in Tunja (state of Boyaca). Her main interest was learning how to serve others—like her mother—but she never related it to religion. Considering her enjoyment of and aptitude for mathematics she was searching for a profession that would put this talent to use. This was somewhat of a problem since

135

she was not particularly interested in medicine, and in those days, it was considered "scandalous" for a girl to be an engineer.

Following her graduation, she returned home and taught at the local grade school. Serving others suddenly loomed as the most important thing in her life and she decided, quite abruptly, to become a nun. After taking her religious vows, Sister Maria Esperanza entered the National University in Bogota to study economics and accounting, transferring after five semesters to the Javeriana University, a Jesuit school.

The idea of "Home-Schools" came to her early in 1975 while she was at the Javeriana. She had been assigned by her religious order, the *"Terciaria Dominica,"* to a school run by the Sisters, in Funza, a low-income neighborhood on the outskirts of Bogota, and along with two other nuns, to develop a program to educate the *"campesinos."* She put her idea on paper and it was approved by the Order the same year.

Living in Funza made it easier to put the program into action because the Sisters were well-acquainted with the *"campesinos"* and the people of the *"barrios."* But she was still pursuing her degree at the Javeriana, studying at night, working to establish the "Home-Schools," and attending classes by day. Although the University had given her a leave of absence for a limited time to enable her to work on the "Home-Schools" program, Maria Esperanza knew she was fast approaching the time when she would have to choose between the two. She could not do both. In the end, there was little decision to be made: a professional career in mathematics no longer mattered. Serving the poor was everything.

From that moment onward, all her working hours have been committed to development of the "Home-Schools." Sister Maria Esperanza has travelled the length and width of Colombia in the process of strengthening the program.

---

[1] *"Barrio"* is the Spanish word used to refer to a *"neighborhood"* or suburban district of town.

SOME SOW, OTHERS REAP

by

Maria Esperanza Briceno

"**D**ear Lord—Please hear my prayer. You know Jose is away in the city looking for work. I haven't heard from him for a long time. I pray, O Lord, that you will protect him and let him come home soon. The corn is ready to harvest and, with the help of the children, I'll try to manage alone. But, O Lord, the crop is very bad this time—it's mildewed and full of worms. There'll scarcely be enough to make the flour for the 'arepas,'[2] but I'll send Joselito to the market to try to sell what we can get along without. Joselito knows he has to take his father's place and he's a good boy. I'm sorry he won't be able to go to school this year—I know he's very disappointed, but he says nothing. He knows he's needed at home and that he's the man of the family until Jose returns.

I don't like to send Joselito to the market alone because he's so young that the buyers won't give him the best price. But what else can I do, O Lord? The baby's sick and will surely die if he has to lie in the damp air of the market all day. Please help him get well, Lord. Don't take him away like you did the others. I promise I'll try to take better care of him. If I could learn to knit sweaters, or maybe to do embroidery—these are things that cost much at the market—· Joselito could sell them when the crops are bad, and I'd at least be able to buy a little medicine for the baby. Please, O lord, you're the only one who can help me."

—A *"campesina's"* prayer.

The area of Facatativa is not very different from many of the villages that dot the Colombian "interior."[3] Its people are good people, they mean well, and they do the best they know how with what they have to work with. The ways of its women are not unlike women's ways everywhere.

A young *"campesina"* being courted is easily swept off her feet by a would-be lover who is adept at sugary words and flattery. Just the other day, I was walking through the park about dusk and happened upon two young lovers sitting on the grass watching the sunset. Both were bashful, but the girl was especially shy. A light blush colored her cheeks and she pretended to be playing with her braids instead of meeting the young man's earnest gaze. I knew that when she made up her mind to look into his eyes, she would believe anything he told her. I was reminded of another young woman, only a little older than she, who came to me not long ago.

The young woman, who I will call Maria, had been recently married and was now with child. Eight months pregnant, Maria knew her husband was spending nights

---

[2]A kind of coarse flat bread which looks like a thick pancake. It is made of corn ground into flour, lard, and water, but includes no seasoning or salt. Baked in an earth oven, *"arepas"* are a staple of the *"campesino"* diet.

[3]The population of Colombia is densest on the the high plateaus, slopes and basins in the western part of the country. These are inland areas where the elevation modifies the effects of Colombia's equatorial climate, the most populated being the Department (State) of Cundinamarca, where Bogota, the capital, is located.

away from home with other women. Although when they were courting, he had told her, "I could never look at another,"—and she had believed him—she was now resigned to her fate. "It will be different when the baby comes," she hoped aloud. One knows, however, that Maria will follow the path of the other women she has known and admired—others who have suffered, martyred themselves to abide by their marriage vows, sacrificed for their families—her mother, her grandmother, the heroine of the radio soap opera. Maria will make excuses for her husband to others and to herself; she will devote herself to her child and do her best to get along without complaining. She will look forward to such things as buying a new "ruana"[4] and going to the city.

Is this true only at the "campesina" level? I think not. It is a trait that is aided, abetted and perpetuated by women at all social levels, but it is especially detrimental to the "campesina." Unlike her middle and upperclass sisters, who at least gain some creature comforts and assurance for their old age, she is obliged to serve as a willing worker twenty-four hours a day, without pay or benefit.

I live with the people of Facatativa; they are my friends and neighbors. If you are an "outsider"[5] it is difficult to become well-acquainted with these rural people, and their ways are often misinterpreted or misunderstood. When the "campesina" is not sure of her situation, she takes refuge in silence. If she feels she has a reason for distrusting someone, a pair of mules could not haul words from her mouth. But much of the time, her reluctance to speak is because of her innate shyness and feeling of inferiority. Most of my friends suffer when they have to greet a stranger; and they find they simply cannot speak their minds if strangers are around. They really believe they do not have a right to an opinion, to make their presence felt, and even less to take part in community decision-making.

Maria, for example, works part-time as a cook on a nearby "hacienda."[6] She tells me her "patron"[7] makes her feel as if she were "less than nothing" and she accepts this as a reality, believing the menfolk should do the talking. "My father got me my job—he told "mi patron" I was a willing worker and didn't ask for time off. He talks to "mi patron" about the cattle and "mi patron" trusts him." It is a man's world.

Maria knows she is expected to be around when she is needed, to serve coffee as often as her "patron" asks for it, do the laundry, pick up all the trash, and in addition to cook three meals a day, to second-guess the wishes of a demanding, thoughtless, and sometimes even cruel master. When the "patron" visits the "hacienda," he spends a great deal of time with the foreman enthusiastically asking about the cows, seeds and fertilizer. He is always concerned about vaccinations of

---

[4]A "ruana" is a kind of cloak worn by most rural people in Colombia. In the highlands, it is made of heavy woolen materials, often homespun, and selected for warmth. It is often used as a blanket. In the lowlands, it is made of lighter material, usually cotton, chosen for color and design.

[5]An "outsider" can refer to anyone not a local resident such as people from the city, even though Colombian. It also includes "campesinos" from other parts of the country, and of course, all foreigners.

[6]An "hacienda" is a large farm, usually an estate that is privately owned.

[7]"Patron" is an employer, landowner, "boss," or any person in a position of power and authority with whom the "campesino" or worker has a direct relationship or is economically dependent. It is usually the term used by a "campesino" or other subordinate to address the person believed to be in control of his/her life—"mi patron," meaning "my master" or "my boss." Traditionally, it was expected that the "campesino" owed his loyalty to the "patron," who in turn, was supposed to provide his workers with a degree of security which would enable them to live at a subsistence level.

the animals, medicine for the calves, and salt for the cattle. It never crosses his mind, however, to inquire about the health of the children, much less the woman who shares the chores of the *"hacienda"* with her husband. How then, can we expect Maria to view herself as a person, a human being of value rather than a "thing," when she knows the animals are more important?

Let me try to describe the background against which life is lived in Facatativa. It is not really a town in the true sense of the word, but rather an area. It begins about 35 kilometers outside of Bogota, the capital, and covers an expanse of the countryside which includes two kinds of land.

The first is a section of the Bogota plateau, situated at an elevation of about 9,000 feet. Because of the altitude, it is generally chilly and often wet with rain. The terrain is well endowed for raising cattle and includes rich pasture lands, but the *"campesinos"* are not the ones who profit from its fertility; on the contrary, the benefits are reaped by the land-owners, while the workers who toil on the land suffer miserably from the harsh weather and never gain more than barely enough to hold body and soul together. The plateau is divided into big cattle ranches and grazing lands whose well-to-do owners live in Bogota. The running of the *"haciendas"* is left to superintendents. The actual farm work is taken care of by the *"campesinos"* who live nearby and work for a pittance as laborers on schedules which recognize no time limits.

The remaining part of the Facatativa area is mostly mountainous—rocky canyons and steep hillsides where the soil is impoverished and eroded. A few poor farmers own small plots of this exhausted land where they eke out an existence with such crops as coffee, corn, sugar cane, fruit and cocoa. Some of the slopes are so vertical, one wonders how the people keep from falling off when they work. The climate here ranges between warm and hot, and the mountainsides are patched with the efforts of these families who, while they own the land, must toil desperately to produce what is indispensable for their survival. There are no roads in this area, no agricultural machinery, no money to buy improved seed or fertilizer.

When I visit the family of Tomasa, I have to travel by jeep for an hour and a half, then walk another two hours. We consider that they live rather close. The drive is slow because most of the way is by a dirt road, usually deep with mud from recent rains. We have to drive carefully because it is easy to hit a pig or cow that may wander across the path, and even skinny chickens are very valuable to their owners. Chickens, however, are usually hobbled to a blade of grass or a bush to prevent their straying. The last time I visited Tomasa's family was after a heavy rain. I trudged up to the little house through the mud, and although it was nearly dusk, I could not detect a light and I was afraid something might have happened to take the family away from home. Suddenly, her twins—two little boys of about 8 or 9—flew out of the house and ran to meet me, each grabbing a hand. "Where is your Mama?" I asked.

Almost as I spoke, their older sister, Caty, appeared in the doorway wiping her hands on a soiled apron. Please notice that I do not describe Caty as a "little" girl. I cannot bring myself to think of her as a child, although she is no more than ten and quite small for her age. One is forced to regard her as a contemporary because she always seems to be carrying the weight of the world on her shoulders. At ten, she is like an old woman.

"Oh, Sister—God be praised—Mama was praying that you'd come." She slapped at her brothers with a rag she had in her hand, shooing them back into the interior of the cottage. "Don't pester Sister," she scolded, and continued to me, in the same breath "Mama is sick—she has a bad cold. Thanks be to God you are here."

The "campesina" has a well-developed, innate sense of religion inherited from her forbearers. She trains her children from earliest childhood, to perform pious practices daily, and imbues them with her own interpretation of faith. She constantly uses expressions such as "with God's help," "God willing," "thanks be to God," "the Lord will repay you" and "if God wills it..." When she is surprised, frightened or happy, she expresses herself with expletives like, "My God!" and "God Bless You!" The children have heard these expressions from the time they can remember, and the words simply become a part of their speech habits.

The little cottage was built partly of adobe and partly with stones collected from the fields. One side was patched up with a piece of rusty corrugated tin. Inside, it was divided into two rooms with a hard clay brick and dirt floor. The first room served as a kitchen, an eating area and general all-purpose living room. In the dim flickering light of a candle on a wooden table, I saw that a pot was hissing over some coals at one end of the room. The coals gave off the only warmth in the damp, chill—more psychological than actual heat. The blackened clay pot was half-filled with cooked corn meal which appeared to be warmed over from a previous meal. A puppy shared the space in the corner with two sickly-looking chickens. The wall that separated the living room from the sleeping area beyond was papered with yellowed newspapers, but decorated with dusty, colored-paper streamers and a paper flower from a previous Christmas or Easter celebration. Another almost depleted candle burned in a dish on a shelf, illuminating a small, sad picture of The Lord Jesus.

Caty led me by the hand through a small doorway covered by a piece of burlap, into the room beyond which had no window and was bathed in darkness. As my eyes became accustomed to the darkness, I saw the mother lying in a dark heap on

e floor covered by an assortment of ragged blankets. Caty stood by holding the candle from the kitchen table, which cast deep ominous shadows in the tiny room.

Tomasa was very ill. Her eyes were hollow and she could not speak without coughing, "Sister, I have been praying you would come. God Bless You! You can help us. Please get word to my sister." The woman had, for some months, been going to the local clinic several miles away where she was given medication for tuberculosis. I saw several small bottles of medicine next to the far wall and picked one up to see what she was taking. To my surprise, I found it was full. All the bottles were unopened. "Why have you not been taking your medicine?" I asked. "The *curandero*[8] says it is evil," she whispered, "He gives me special things that are better."

While the *"campesina"* attempts to translate her spiritual sense into everyday, living situations, the means often fail her. Sensing this failure, she falls back on her "inherited" religiosity which also includes the superstitions she inherited from her mother and her mother before her. She will consult the *"curandero"* of the area and accept his advice *without* question and follow his instructions to the letter. She will hang on to tradition, oblivious to its possible meaning, reacting negatively to change, not listening to reason. Only tradition is "good." Innovation is regarded with fear and distrust.

Although the *"campesinas"* attend Church services, their attitude is one of being present at a magic ritual, a ceremony one must attend or run the risk of being punished by an unseen God, but at the same time, not really understanding it. They are always concerned about their own practice of the rituals, perceiving the practice as an obligation rather than an expression of belief.

I often see *"campesinas"* walk into Church carrying their children with others close behind, sit down, make themselves comfortable and simply observe the ceremony while the children play on the floor. They remain for as long as it takes their husbands to do the shopping and take care of their business. It is a way to spend some time resting in quiet and safe surroundings.

As with most *"campesinas,"* Tomasa was not aware that her "feeling poorly" from the *"grippe"*[9] required bed rest. She was convinced she had been born to work until she drew her last breath, and accordingly, did not lie down until she could no longer stand up. The *"campesina"* will undergo privations and all kinds of pain and discomfort without complaining. In many cases, when the woman finally lies down because she is "very sick," she is actually at "death's door." It is too late for help.

In the face of family death, the *"campesina"* is stoic. She shows her grief by wearing black clothing and by not appearing in public. She will often continue to wear black for the remainder of her life, visiting the cemetery as often as she can, taking flowers and praying devotedly for the dead.

Consider then what life would be like for the child, Caty, if her mother died. She has already been taught to take her homemaking role very seriously. She has

---

A person believed knowledgeable about and capable of overcoming spells cast by witchcraft, the *"curandero"* diagnoses and treats ailments that fall into the natural or supernatural category, the line of distinction being blurred. Treatment may involve complex, spiritualistic-type methods, and in some cases, *"curanderos"* demonstrate considerable knowledge of folk medicine, particularly the curative uses of herbs.

The uneducated often use the term *"grippe,"* meaning influenza, to refer to aches, pains and other symptoms of a bad cold.

attained skill in washing clothes for the entire family including her two brothers and father when he is not "away working." The laundry is done once a week in a nearby river where she and her mother spend the day in the water, barefooted, with their skirts and sleeves rolled up, beating home-made soap into the worn fabrics on the rocks. The clothes are carried home and spread out to dry on bushes near the house where they can be gathered quickly if it rains, which it does frequently.

Caty already spends much of her time in the dark kitchen with four stones for a stove, and only a few clay pots and wooden spoons for cooking. The only water for drinking and cooking is that she and her brothers carry in jugs from the river which is several city blocks away. Bathing is also done in the river. Is it any wonder that local superstitions abound such as "it is dangerous to bathe more than once every week or two," and "the night air is full of evil spirits that make you sick!"

Tomasa has taught Caty to mend the family clothes, but they have been too poor to ever consider buying a sewing machine. Tomasa has tried to keep the children neat, but it is not easy. If she were to die, the responsibility for making a home for the children and the father would fall completely to Caty. It would put an end to her already slim hope of attending school. And yet, this is the fate of many girls in Colombia. It is the record of our underdevelopment, the backwardness of hundreds of years, a total existence on the margin of life. The ignorance suffered by our "campesinas" does not even allow them to perceive as needs many of the so-called necessities required by educated women with different lifestyles.

The rural women work shoulder to shoulder with the men when there is need. They have no inkling of the latest inventions of modern technology. There is seldom electricity in the villages, so they have no idea what it is like to have a refrigerator, a washing machine, an electric iron or a water heater, much less a toilet that flushes, a bathtub or shower with hot and cold running water or a television set. A transistor or battery radio is their recreation, but luck is such that the man of the family usually takes it with him to work. Consequently, they are able to listen to it only during the hours he is home, when the broadcasts are mainly news—which it can be said in passing, does not interest them at all. Newspapers never reach their villages—the idea of the "paper" being delivered daily to their door would probably make them break out in laughter. Their vocabularies are extremely limited, and knowledge of the world beyond the local village is so meagre as to be almost non-existent.

Life for the "campesina" revolves around her children, her husband and her immediate family which often includes parents, grandparents or other relatives who may come to live in her home. She has acquired such tremendous patience over her hundreds of years of servitude, that society now regards it as a characteristic trait of the rural woman, rather than a virtue, and she is often mistakenly viewed as "dense" or "stolid." Because the family forms the center of her value system, she puts up with a critical mother-in-law, a nagging mother, nurses a senile grandfather, or a drunken and often abusive husband. Some combination of such members of the family frequently live under her roof. Her patience all too often makes it possible for her to lead the drunken husband home, uncomplaining, after his day at the market, or playing "tejo"[10] at the village pool hall. But, what she

---

[10]A game played by rural men, usually at the "tienda," the village's all-purpose store or pool-hall. It is played on an out-door court, by teams, and is closely associated with beer-drinking, which is the main function of the establishment. "Tejo" is pursued with great excitement and earnestness, the losers prorating among themselves the cost of the beer consumed. The "tienda" is open during the evening hours, but usually is crowded only on Saturdays and Sundays when the "campesinos" arrive early and stay late.

would give not to have to bring him home, knowing that as soon as they arrive he will beat her or demand that which she cannot give!

With the family as the center of her universe, she respects the responsibilities of god-parenting, places a high value on friendships, and ignores envy and selfishness. Unfortunately, the "campesina" holds in high esteem any person she believes knows more than she, or who is "better off," economically. Any social life beyond the family usually is connected to village affairs. The "campesina" enjoys working in community activities such as bazaars and "fiestas"[11] to raise money for local projects.

On these occasions it is traditional for women to remain in the kitchen to take care of the food and serve. Nevertheless, they follow in great detail the results of sales, and bring great pressure on making good use of the funds collected. Values are such that the fortunate "campesina" is one who basks in importance when her husband belongs to a community organization or when her children play some role in school activities.

The rural woman's role is an essential one in the life of the family, although if we analyze her impact on family finances we might say that she does not actually produce. Rather, her labor reduces family expense. That is to say that she is gainfully unemployed.

Our "campesina" does not handle money, although when her husband's back is turned, she may conduct business on the side, such as selling a few eggs, maybe a chicken, or a few pounds of whatever harvest is left over, to the neighbors. The proceeds may simply be bartered goods, but hopefully, she will gain a few pennies to stash away to hedge against unforseen expenses, since her husband never gives her enough. In this way she manages to save a few "pesos"[12] she can use to buy medicine for the sick child, buy baby clothes, pay for pencils and a notebook to enable a child to go to school, or perhaps to pay a neighbor to help with the laundry and cook during the week her baby is born.

Many women have turned to making handcrafted items, especially in areas where raw materials are at hand. They weave straw into baskets, hats and handbags; and use sisal to make slippers, feedbags and cinches for horses. Those who live on the plateau often spin raw wool into yarn, then weave it into "ruanas," shawls of various sizes, and caps. Sometimes, the entire family becomes involved, particularly in the making of clay products such as flowerpots, cooking pots and platters, water jugs and containers for "arepas"—even dolls. Many "campesinas" are very creative and seem to have inherited a natural attraction for music, dancing and folklore which, when integrated into their handicrafts, become quite marketable. Generally, whatever small income they are able to bring in with these efforts is a result of time spent over and above that demanded by their daily chores; consequently, it is a sideline activity.

Keep in mind that since there is no electricity, work begins at daylight and ceases at nightfall. This kind of work is difficult in that the woman usually has no financial

---

[11] "Fiestas" are religious or state holidays celebrated to commemorate important events such as the birth or death of a saint.

[12] The "peso" is the unit of monetary exchange in Colombia. It is presently (1980) valued at about U.S. $.0222.

resources with which to begin—to buy raw materials. It is also a problem to get transportation to and from the market just to find the needed materials. Even in the areas where the raw materials are readily at hand, other basic items for producing the handicraft must be purchased.

Other drawbacks are the limited demand for handcrafted items that cannot be produced in great quantities, and the competition in other areas. If the handicraft is the result of part-time pursuit, it is almost mandatory that it be created for neighbors or the local village market. Obviously, this limits what can be earned from producing the article. On the other hand, it does not smother creativity; perhaps it may even be a factor in stimulating more imaginative work. And in any case, as long as production is for the neighbors and the local market, there is less of a problem of the profits being siphoned off by "middlemen."

Seeing the need that exists was how my work began. I founded the program for "Home Schools" in 1975 after having worked with rural people near Funza, where I lived for several years while I was studying at the university. "Home-Schools" began as an education project for *"campesinos,"* and is now a legally registered private non-profit organization. It is not for women only. Its main purpose is to prepare the rural family to improve its living conditions through community self-help.

"Home-Schools" offer courses to community groups in literacy (first to fifth grade level), cooking, first-aid, sewing, knitting, vegetable gardening, ethics (religion), principles of cooperativism, and rural administration. The courses are run by the community people, themselves, using tape recorders, audio cassettes and slide projectors in coordination with simply written, illustrated booklets. That is to say, the *"campesinos"* provide the place and the course leaders; "Home-Schools" provides the media.

We begin by motivating the individual families to take action, as a community, to organize the "Home-School" centers. We took our name because the "school room" or meeting place is usually supplied by one of the families. It can be a storeroom, a shed or any extra space that is large enough to accomodate 30-40 people. The "students" are often entire families—mothers, who come carrying their babies, fathers, teen-agers, and pre-teenaged youngsters—even the grandparents. The courses are usually in the evenings at the end of the workday, so everybody can attend. Once they are motivated, the groups select the course moderators (coordinators). The community decides how often they will meet, and how long the meetings will last. Step by step, the group acquires the decision-making ability to choose the content of the program.

We say that "Home-Schools" offer "integrated" education. This is our way of saying that we try to offer specific information in designated course study areas, but that the information goes beyond the boundaries of the specific courses of study. Each School meeting includes a discussion of one or more of the following areas as they relate to the specific course the group has elected to study:

1) **Professional training** and how to gain access to it;
2) **Local habits in nutrition, hygiene, health and recreation,** and how they can be improved;

---

[13]*"Hogar-Escuelas"* is registered with the Colombian government.

3) **Income-generating projects** within the constraints of the local community's economic climate (agricultural or cattle-raising);
4) **Local traditions and customs:** understanding their heritage, developing it, using it, and taking pride in it.

The specific courses offered and the above areas which are integrated into them are further focused on family and community; work and recreation; math, reading and writing at different levels; and religion.

By the time the group has completed a course, the community usually has organized to carry out a concrete project in which it will apply the new knowledge. These projects are almost always related to increasing income.

The traditional role of the *"campesina"* is that of a working partner, but as I stated earlier, she has no control of the money. Women are becoming aware through our courses, however, that opportunities exist for them to earn money by acquiring extra skills. Dress-maker's shops, hand-knitted articles, and hand-woven rugs are beginning to appear in some of the villages; in others, women trained in first-aid are earning extra money by serving the community. It remains a problem for dress-makers to acquire sewing machines; for others to get the necessary yarn and thread for knitting and weaving; and needed medicines, drugs and instruments for paramedics. Sometimes, it seems there are so many problems that one hardly knows where to begin first.

You the reader, may well ask, "Why are the 'Home-Schools' teaching such irrelevant things for which the rural woman seldom can even buy the raw materials to begin?" It is a logical question and it has been asked many times before. "Home-Schools," asks the question of itself. We find ourselves answering the question with others: Do we have the right to deny to a community the kind of help it requests for the problems it views as its most important? Can we ignore the desperate need of the *"campesina"* to earn a few pennies for the emergency which is sure to come, knowing all the while it is not a "long-term solution" to her problems?

Actually, we are seeking both long-term and short-term solutions. "Home-Schools" has begun bringing groups of approximately twenty-four *"campesinas"* at a time to intern at our headquarters in Funza. They stay for periods of about two months each. We have found this to be very helpful to the women, as well as to ourselves: living together for two months permits a degree of intimacy that is necessary to get to the bottom of their problems and respond to their needs. At the same time, it is making it possible for us to train them to go home and disseminate to other women what they have learned. They have a tremendous potential for changing those old superstitions and habits that hold them back. While the *"campesina"* has great influence on her family, she suffers from the effects of *"machismo"*[14] often without being aware of it. She worries a great deal about her brothers, and her concern over the whims of her father often overshadows all else. *"Machismo"* is very deceptive and difficult to grapple with.

For example, a number of the women do not think they can work the earth. Many

---

[14]Traits of the ideal male are referred to as *"machismo,"* and the closer a man comes to reaching the ideal, the more *"macho"* he is said to be. The essence of these traits, at the personal level, is embodied by demonstration of sexual prowess; amatory success with women and large families serve to affirm a man's masculinity. Other characteristics of the ideal which are universally admired are physical strength, self-assurance, aggressiveness, daring and adventurousness, and the ability to speak well and forcefully.

feel their place is to have babies, look after the family, and especially to see that the men are fed. Of course, this includes grinding the corn and coffee which, during harvest season is a formidable job, particularly if you are also caring for four or five children. Consequently, it is sometimes difficult to persuade them to grow vegetables which they desperately need to supplement their starchy diets. We provide seeds for vegetables and teach those who are interested how to cultivate them. We have found we can motivate them by linking the vegetables to feeding rabbits. While they like to eat rabbit, most think they can't raise them because grain is so expensive or unavailable. Initially we tell them the seeds are for radishes and carrots which are excellent for feeding rabbits; and we give them a pair of rabbits. They then will make a great effort to raise the vegetables, feeling that this is a part of their duty to put food on the table for the men. Little by little, we show them how to prepare the vegetables so the family, as well as the rabbits, can eat them.

My greatest desire is that the "campesino," both man and woman, feel a greater sense of themselves, of their own person; and that upon gaining this sense, will see the need to work more closely with the other members of the community. I pray that we will be able to provide them with the kind of social workshops they need. I pray that we can help them to establish community centers where they can work voluntarily on collaborative projects that will benefit the entire area. I pray that the rural family will not leave home for the city streets, and that it will have a good reason to stay: more economic access to goods and services, more social justice, more dignity, more time for each other and for friends. I pray that we can lead the "campesina" to discover her own value and awaken her to a new world. And I pray that those of us who have discovered who we are will struggle on behalf of those who have not yet learned they are human. I call on you, dear reader, to reflect with me so that, together, we may explore new ideas, search for answers, and discover the resources which surely exist to make this a better and more just world for those who have yet to enjoy its benefits.

THE BROKEN WING

Jenny Valcarcel Arce (Peru)

Jenny Valcarcel Arce can be found almost every evening at the cramped upstairs offices of the Center for Guidance and Human Development (COPH) in downtown Lima. The outer office is crowded with working-class men and women waiting to enroll in courses given free of charge at the Center. During the day, Jenny holds a part-time position with the Advisory Council of the Ministry of Education, and another as the Peruvian representative to the International Institute of Integration's Study Commission. But it is at COPH, where she volunteers her services as a "technical advisor" to work with rural women who have migrated to Lima and young people, that her eyes sparkle and her face comes alive with enthusiasm. Although she speaks with a quiet voice, almost one of humility, one nevertheless feels her inner strength and independence.

If Jenny is not at COPH, they will know where to find her. In the past several years, she has taken special assignments in Bolivia, Venezuela, Colombia and Chile. She spent most of 1979 in Bolivia giving short non-formal education courses in Cochabamba and Santa Cruz. As she says, "I have made a strong Christian and social commitment to my work, and I have no family to tie me down."

Jenny was born in Puno and spent her earliest years in the area of Lake Titicaca, the highest lake in the world. At age 5, she moved with her family to Arequipa, a colonial town founded in 1540 by Pizarro, at the base of six active volcanoes.

Although her mother played a traditional role in the home, both parents had a strong desire that each of their three children become educated and pursue a profession. Her father, involved in local industry, believed that women as well as men should cultivate their minds, not only to stand up for their rights, but also to develop their ability to help others for the benefit of all mankind. Jenny is convinced that people who live in the Andes have a special awareness of human pain and difficulties because of their own suffering, first as victims of volcanic eruptions—then, at the hands of the Spanish conquistadores. Her parents' interest in local history was passed on to Jenny, in whom it took root and flowered into human compassion and concern for others.

Following high school in Arequipa, Jenny attended Catholic University in Lima where she earned a degree in Social Science, a doctorate in Education, and another degree in Journalism and Communication Science. Her interest was to prepare herself to be of the greatest possible service to others, and led to postgraduate studies at the University of Milan, the Gregorian University in Rome, the universities of Madrid and Barcelona, Texas and Miami, and in Belgium. She then returned to Peru to put into practice what she had learned.

Professionally, Jenny considers herself an educator and journalist who uses her talents where she feels they will do the most good. Sometimes it is helping to plan the eduational system of the country; sometimes she is a guidance counsellor; other times she acts as a technical advisor to organizations involved in non-formal education. What she enjoys most is action-oriented work where she can be in direct contact with the *"campesina."* Her early contact with the suffering of the poor women of the Andes has provided a foundation on which her interest in developing the potential of all Latin American women is based. She gives much credit to Dr. Gabriela Anibar of the Inter-American Commission of Women, for opening her eyes to the relationship of underdevelopment to the unpreparedness and activities of women.

What are Jenny's plans for the future? She will tell you she is interested in reminding governments and organizations that are implementing agricultural programs for *"campesinos,"* not to forget the feminine sector. "You know, the men don't build those irrigation canals and cultivate the wheat by themselves! More than half the work is done by women. Yet, who gets the technical training?"

Up front in Jenny's future is a project she is planning to initiate in the Peruvian areas of the Amazon jungle. Her eyes light up and she looks directly at you. "I can't do it alone—but here's an area where our Peruvian system of education is useless. The people of the jungle have fabulous abilities and practical knowledge, but nothing we are doing there is really appropriate. I want to develop a special non-formal program, a kind of 'frontier' education that will be totally dedicated to giving these people an opportunity to make more of their lives."

THE BROKEN WING
by
Jenny Valcarcel Arce

I was born and raised in the Andes. Since my earliest childhood, the suffering of the *"serrana"*[1] and her children has been indelibly etched on my mind. I am of these people, but I am one of the fortunate few. I was able to obtain an education, and because of this I feel I have the right and the responsibility to speak out.

In Latin America, we have a tremendous need to study the problems presented by the feminine half of the population, particularly those who exist on the margin of society. In Peru, the majority is chained by the inability to read and write, by unemployment. Even more pernicious is the fact that woman is regarded as a thing of pleasure, as nothing more than a servile support to the male ego. Seldom is she seen as a companion and a person who should participate in making any decisions. The decisions on how our country is developed are being made and have always been made by the "other half." Over time, this has resulted in disassociating the woman from worth as a human being—unfortunately even in her own mind. This condition has settled heavily on the *"campesina."*[2] She has become the "broken wing" of our society.

The *"campesina"* greatly distrusts those whom she does not know; it is a suspicion borne of poverty, timidity, diffidence and lack of opportunity for knowledge. She especially distrusts city people, seeing them as "persons who come to exploit us and use our problems against us."

Now that I am educated and viewed as someone from the "Capital," it is often difficult for me to convince *"campesinas"* that I want to help them. However, once the "ice is broken," the first layer penetrated, I encounter an exceedingly rich philosophy and psychological understanding in these rural women. Believe me, they can compete with any cultured urban woman in the areas of human sensitivity, level of values, and family dignity. If our culture permits the rural woman to remain on the margin of society, perpetuating her deplorably detrimental status, the work of pushing our country into the 21st century will be doubled.

Not long ago, I was in an Andean village where I was offered a place to stay by a family that had a maidservant. My concern for the underprivileged rural woman made me extremely aware of two distinctly different attitudes exhibited by the lady of the house. The first was one of diplomacy, receptivity and openness—education —reflecting her position in a family of means residing in the sierra and a hostess to one of her "own class" from the city. At the same time, I could not help noticing her different attitude toward the maid; one of hostility, of rejection.

The servant, a bright-eyed local girl no more than 18 or 20 years old, was, according to my hostess, "an ugly little thing",..."not worth a pin"..."ignorant"..."an

---

[1] In Peru, people from the Andes region refer to themselves as *"serranos"* rather than *"campesinos"* (country folk), *"indios"* (Indians), or *"montaneros"* (mountaineers or mountain folk).

[2] *"Campesina,"* indicating a rural woman; can include both mountain women and women from the jungle.

idiot." Nevertheless, the girl had a penetrating way of looking at you—an alive look—that impressed me. In the few moments that my hostess saw me engage the girl in conversation, she made a great "to-do" over my talking with her, believing that although she was beneath me, I was doing her a great favor by giving her my attention. My interest, she was certain, stemmed from my "research on 'campesinas.'" The truth is that I really was interested in learning about the girl, in knowing her for herself.

It turned out that she was the oldest of nine children, that she and her mother, a widow, were charged with raising the family alone in a small cottage somewhere in the hills nearby. I have seldom known anyone who had such a strong sense of responsibility for her family as this young woman—albeit, that she had no educa-tion, could not read or write, and was so very poor. She told me, "When my brothers and sisters grow up, I want them to be somebody. I'd give my life to see that they're not treated as I've been. I want them to study, to learn, to have a career in the Capital, and when they return to the sierra, to be respected. I'm a kind of slave although I hear people say that slavery is dead. If this is so, I don't want its ghost to haunt my brothers and sisters the way it haunts me!"

In spite of the inferior status assigned her and living all her life in an isolated mountain village, it was obvious that she was unusually intelligent. I was impressed by the fact that she showed no resentment toward her "patrones,"[3] a common at-titude among many of the maidservants I have come to know.

During my stay, I visited the local grade school and made arrangements for the girl to learn to read and write. Some two years later I had occasion to return to this small town and looked her up. I found that with the small amount of education she had received, she had been motivated to open a little shop that her mother took care of. Although she continued to work as a domestic servant to add to the family income, her salary, together with earnings from the store, enabled her to send the younger children to school. I was amazed when she told me, "'Senorita,' I am trying to help other girls who are abused by their 'patrones.' I sit them in a chair at the shop and I give them advice. I tell them that there's nothing wrong with being a worker, but they can improve themselves, and they must never let people mistreat them. I know, because I, too, am a maid. And they listen to me."

The story of this girl is unusual only in the sense that she was given an oppor-tunity—someone helped her "open the door." Aside from this meagre assistance which was all she needed, the rest she did by herself. My awareness of this latent strength and capability of the "campesina" is what impels me to devote all my time—paid, as well as an unpaid volunteer—to mending the "broken wing" of our society.

One of my most vivid experiences was a kind of seminar I gave—a "cursillo,"[4] we call it—for a group of women ranging in ages from 16-60. The course involved one meeting per week over about 10 weeks and revolved around making each woman aware of her own reality, her own abilities. Individual meetings had different themes, but each was interspersed with information about geography, civics and

---

[3]The term "patron" is commonly used in Peru by domestic servants, rural laborers, and others from the "blue-collar" working class, in reference to employers. A literal translation of the word is "master."

[4]A "cursillo" is a short course, usually devoted to some kind of informal, adult learning.

natural science. It was carried out free of charge under the sponsorship of the Guidance and Human Development Center (COPH), a private non-profit Peruvian organization located in Lima. The only prerequisite was that the women be domestic servants. Two important factors have led us to conduct these and similar "cursillos." One is the knowledge that a major underlying cause of the underdevelopment of Latin America is the low socio-cultural integration of the rural and urban women who just exist, living on the margin of society. These women have been unable to integrate themselves or fully contribute to the improvement of the community, either as individuals or as an equal partner of the "human couple." The second is our realization that neither the country at large nor the woman on the threshold of Peruvian society is aware of the reality in which she lives or her potential. She has been discounted because of her illiteracy and timidity. Her lack of confidence is over-powering. The process of bringing her "out of her shell" is, therefore, very slow and must be done with great sensitivity and care.

The meetings of the "cursillo" took place at the Center's adult education classroom in Lima. I found myself with about 40 women, the majority of whom were from the interior of the country, mostly the sierra. In order to persuade them to trust me, I made an effort to get them to identify with me. I told them I shared with them all the nostalgic memories of the highlands; that I, too, was a "serrana;" and that I called Puno and Arequipa "home." To "break the ice," I asked each to identify herself and tell where she was from.

"Now, I would like to hear about your hometown. Is there anyone here from my 'pueblo?'" Several hands were timidly raised, but it was clear that they felt very uncomfortable and mistrust was written all over their faces. I could almost feel the introversion in the way they avoided meeting my eyes, in the way they sat with their heads slightly bowed.

"Don't you agree it's the nicest place in the world?" I asked . This brought a scattered response of giggles, but they had real language difficulty and spoke shyly in a mixture of Spanish with Quechua or Aymara.[5] Nevertheless, they all seemed to relax a little with the knowledge that I, at least, came from their part of the world. Each gave the name of her village and hesitatingly listed some of its beauties.

I hung up a large map of Peru on the wall and together we stuck colored pins in the places they identified. Only three were from Lima. I heard a friendly murmur between several of the women and it appeared that a spark of interest had been raised in knowing each other. The group had begun to warm up.

The second meeting was designed to motivate the group. I knew them all by their first names now and requested that they call me Jenny. They continued calling me "'Senorita' Jenny," an indication that they still felt some distance between their status and mine. For the time being, I ignored it.

Referring to the map we had placed on the wall during the first meeting, I asked them to recall our discussion. I began the session: "Peru, my friends, is not a map, not just a piece of cardboard with names of places on it where we can stick pins to

---

[5]Languages of the Quechua and Aymara people, Amerindians who were among the dominant elements of the Inca Empire. Quechua is widely spoken among present day Indians of the Andes in Peru, Bolivia, Ecuador and Colombia; Aymara is spoken less, mainly in Peru and Bolivia.

show where we come from. It is a living body of which we are a part—it is made up of all of us and many more like us. Our individual problems are the problems of the whole country, like if you have a rock in your shoe it makes you uncomfortable all over. And the problems and difficulties of the country, at the same time, also affect each and every one of you—and me—and all the other people who live in Peru. For example, when it is very cold outside, it makes your nose run, your feet uncomfortable, your hands stiff and your whole body shivers. So you see, if you have great sorrows or great happiness, or if you fail or triumph—Peru also fails or triumphs."

I tried to explain to them that school is for the purpose of recognizing, confronting and solving problems. I told them that the first assignment of this course was to "discover and recognize" their own problems. "Do we have problems? Few, many? Are some more urgent than others? Which are these? Is it important to recognize them? I want you to think about your problems; first—just secretly. Then, I want us to share our problems with the whole group so that we can study them together and help each other." The room buzzed with murmurings of the women, to each other and to everyone in general. It had the sound of general acceptance of my suggestion.

During the third meeting, I explained there were many ways of studying problems. "One way we will do it is by playing a little game. The first time, we are going to have a group rehearsal—then we are each going to play the game by ourselves, individually, privately, and in writing." I asked for a volunteer to begin.

Dorotea, a young woman with her hair braided in pig-tails, shyly raised her hand in an offer to start. "The objective of the game," I told them, "is to guess whether Dorotea prefers salty foods or sweet foods. As I name certain foods, some of which are salty—others sweet—Dorotea is going to raise her fingers according to how well she likes the foods. If it's just a little, she will raise only one finger. If it's more than a little, two or three fingers; much, four fingers; and a whole lot, five." I drew two columns with chalk on the blackboard—one for sweet foods, the other for salty—and showed them that one dot signified one finger, two dots two fingers, and so on. Then the game began.

I named many different foods I knew to be staples of the "campesino" diet, as well as others that they ate only upon special occasion. Dorotea obligingly raised her fingers accordingly, among tittering and giggles, while I indicated in one column or the other, the number of fingers raised. Everyone was enjoying themselves.

When we had completed two columns of foods, I totaled up the dots in each separate column—taking advantage of the opportunity to teach them the numbers from 1 to 5. The final results were 20 points for sweet foods and 11 for salty, as follows:

Chocolate	5	Avocado	2
Cookies	3	Salad	1
Caramels	5	"Anticuchos"[6]	5
Ice Cream	5	Potatoes & Fried Egg	2
Gelatine	2	Cheese with Corn	1
	20		11

---

[6]Small pieces of beef heart barbecued on skewers over charcoal, and eaten with a sauce of pureed or ground fresh yellow chili peppers.

Everyone was laughing, gently teasing Dorotea about her weight and asking if she suffered from indigestion. She took it in good spirit and kidded them back. The game had served its purpose well and I jumped at the opportunity to open the door a little wider to basic information about nutrition.

At the next meeting, we picked up where we had left off. I told them we were going to continue the game but this time, we would not use foods nor would it be a public exhibition. "We will discuss our thoughts and things that bother us, and because these are very serious for each of us, we must keep the discussion very, very private. Instead of talking about salty and sweet foods, I want us to make an impersonal list of possible problems that we face as a group."

They started out very timidly. An older woman in the group said softly, "It could be a group problem of wanting to be able to read and write letters." Another suggested, "Also, the problem of backaches and feeling tired." Gradually, the level of their voices raised and they became more excited as they began to reinforce each other's feelings. "The problems of the bad water here in Lima and the prepared foods that make us sick!" "How about the problem of the Social Security that they don't pay us!" "The problem of wanting to rent a room to live in and be independent!"

Carefully writing these opinions on the blackboard I asked finally, "Any more—anyone else want to add a problem?"

A shy voice came from the back of the room, "Maybe it's also a problem, 'senorita,' this thing of being able to converse—even more, of not being able to converse?"

I asked for a clarification of what she meant, and the group all came to her aid: "The problem of not being able to speak easily with the 'patrona','"[7] several piped in to help her out. This was accompanied by a discernible buzzing whisper of accord from the others. Another added, "And the problem of not having anyone to talk to here because all our friends are back home in the village!" One by one, as the women spilled out their problems, a small ember of kinship began to glow among them. Their common problems that formed this glimmer of warmth became the focal point of our remaining meetings. I fanned the flame to forge a tie that would bind them together and help them to strengthen each other.

I again told the group the game we were going to play was much like the one we played with sweet and salty foods. "This time, however," I explained, "we're each going to use a pencil to put our marks on a piece of paper I will give you," as I passed out paper and pencil to each. Then I called their attention to the six "boxes" on the blackboard, stressing the written word for the color of each, and the numbers. I said, "Each box represents one of the problem areas we discussed last time," and repeated them.

"We're each going to divide the paper I gave you into six parts. Each part will represent one of the problems we discussed." I showed them how to fold the paper in half and demonstrated how it could be torn if it was held against a straight edge.

---

[7]Lady of the house.

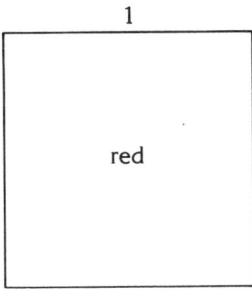

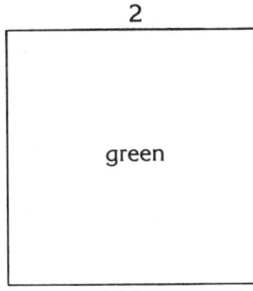

1	2	3
red	green	yellow
Health & Foods	Living Conditions and Housing	Working Conditions and Employment

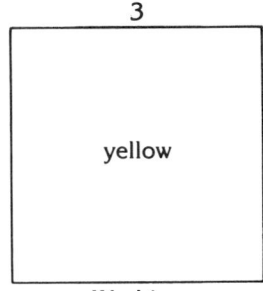

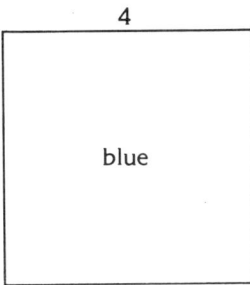

4	5	6
blue	brown	orange
No Opportunity to Study	Unable to Converse with Employers	Lack of Friends

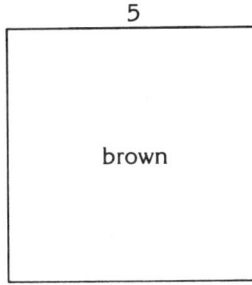

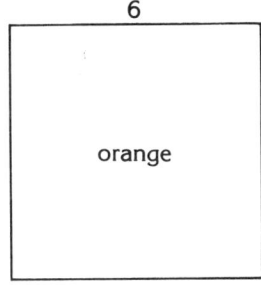

"Now, how're we going to divide and fold the paper into six equal parts? Does anyone have any suggestions?" I was beginning to teach them something about fractions.

They looked puzzled until someone said. "Why don't we pretend it's a piece of cloth and that we're trying to make six matching napkins?" Everyone understood this simple solution. Apparently, it was a dilemma most all had confronted at some time.

When each had folded her sheet of paper into six equal parts, I explained how we would play the game. "I am going to ask a lot of questions. Each time I ask one, I want you to think a moment, and then place a mark with your pencil—like we did before—in the box where you think it belongs." I demonstrated on the blackboard.

"If you feel the answer is 'no, I have never had any problems with this,' instead of a line, make a zero, like this." And I drew a "O" on the blackboard. "If you think you might have a problem with this, but aren't sure, write only one mark; for a little problem that you have once in a while, two marks; often have problems with, three marks; for regular problems you have everyday, four marks; and for the most serious problems—those that never go away, five marks."

155

We spent the rest of the meeting practicing making marks and my showing them which box was which. They learned to recognize numbers from 0 to 6, the correct names of six colors, and had begun learning to identify the written words for their problems. In the beginning, they had trouble distinguishing which box belonged to which problem; and many had difficulty in actually picking up the pencil and learning to hold it. By the end of the day, most had mastered the pencil and all were excited about the new game.

I did not implement the questionnaire until the next meeting. As I entered the room, there was an attitude of expectancy. We now had arrived at the heart of the workshop: learning to analyze one's own situation as it relates to the rest of society.

The questionnaire covered the following 30 statements:

1. I wish I knew how to read and write.
2. The place where I live is very bad; there is a danger that the walls or roof might fall in.
3. I continually feel ill, but I don't know why. I am always tired.
4. I am bored by my work, I don't like it, and I would like to change jobs.
5. It causes so many problems when I try to talk to my employers that it is not worthwhile. I simply cannot make myself understood.
6. I feel very lonely in my work. I would like to have friends, but my employers do not allow it.
7. I wish I could finish the primary grades.
8. I am not able to keep up on paying my rent and I am afraid they will throw me out.
9. One or more of the following parts of my body almost always ache: throat, shoulder, head, stomach.
10. I am concerned because I do not know my legal rights or which things are due to me as social benefits of my work.
11. My employers don't know of my problems, nor are they interested in finding out.
12. I am cut off from my hometown, from my people.
13. I wish I could complete all the primary grades.
14. I suffer many discomforts; I sleep on the floor. I have no room for my personal belongings.
15. My hands hurt, my fingers are raw and burned from continually being in hot water.
16. I must keep quiet and endure the mistreatment I receive from my employers because I am afraid they will fire me if I complain.
17. My employers never ask me how I am getting along or why I am sad.
18. I am estranged from my parents, brothers and sisters and acquaintances.
19. I wish I could study for a trade or a craft.
20. I have no water, sewage, bathroom facilities or shower where I live.
21. I have a constant itch between my toes, my fingers and under my arms.
22. Although I have no insurance, I would like to have, but my employers have done nothing about it.
23. When my employers scold me for something I should not be blamed for, I would like to able to explain, but I can't. They won't listen and they don't understand.
24. I have had no news from my family. I don't know if they are well or sick, if they have banished me or not.
25. I wish I could study to learn a profession.
26. I am looking for a little room to rent.
27. I am not accustomed to the ways of eating here; as a result, I have lost weight.

28. I never am allowed any days off.
29. When I contradict or question something, I am considered insolent, so I am afraid to say anything to my employers. As a result, they say I don't know how to speak.
30. I am lonely because I have no girlfriends from the area where my home is, with whom I can visit or go out with in the evenings or on Sundays. I have no boyfriends either.

There were actually five questions for each of the six problem areas, but I carefully mixed them in an effort to get a true picture.

When I finished reading all the statements, I told them, "I want each of you to look at your six 'boxes' and observe which one has received the most marks. It's that little box that holds your greatest burden and which only you can do something to change." For those who wanted to discuss the results, I offered to talk to each woman personally. At the end of the meeting, the entire group had lined up for individual discussions.

I asked if they would like to know more about each other's problems and study the combined results of the entire group. Everyone was curious and enthusiastic. In order to study the results of the questionnaire, it was, of course, necessary to collect the six pieces of paper belonging to each participant. I offered to return the papers to everyone who wished to have them back if each would put some sort of identification on her own. Everyone wanted the papers back, but since no one could write, how could they identify them?

SAMPLE ANSWERS

	PSEUDONYM
1 Red: Studying	/ / / - / / / / - / / / / - / / - / /
2 Green: Housing Conditions	/ - O - / / - / / / - /
3 Yellow: Health	/ / / / - / / / - / / / - / - / / / / /
4 Blue: Working Conditions	/ / - / / / - / / / / - / / / / / - / / / / /
5 Brown: Ability to Communicate	/ / / / / - / / / / / - / / / / / - / / / / / - / / / /
6 Orange: Friendship	/ / - / / / / / - / / / - / / / / / - / / / /

There were many suggestions. "Attach a photo," one said. Another suggested, "How about your thumbprint?" It was finally decided that each would invent a little figure or a symbol to represent herself which she would draw on the upper right-hand corner of the papers.

A group of the women volunteered to gather up the papers and tally the responses. This presented another dilemma. Before we could add up the responses, they would have to learn to count. It was amazing to realize that the hunger of these women for knowledge, plus their very human desire to know more about themselves, was the key that enabled them to learn to count. Before the meeting was over, they had not only learned all the numbers up to 100 and the concept of adding and multiplying, but had also summed the totals of the individual "boxes" and arrived at a grand total in each of the six problem areas. The entire group had worked themselves up to a fever pitch of excitement, and would have happily protracted the meeting into the night. I suggested, however, that between then and the following week, that each give much thought to her own scores, and what they meant. We left the group analysis for the next session.

An air of expectancy greeted me as I arrived for the eighth meeting. The women sat in a semi-circle around the blackboard. I took the occasion to say I thought that each person was entitled to his or her own set of problems, as well as the right and responsibility to deal with them in the best way possible. "And there's nothing wrong with seeking advice or looking for help when you need it," I added. "It's also important to know—as you've discovered here—that every group, every village, every neighborhood, has one or more general problems that're common to everyone. The problem is well on the way to being solved if the group recognizes it exists, studies it together, and everyone works together in an effort to confront the situation that affects each individual. This is one of the things we're going to begin doing today."

I then placed the meeting in the hands of the women who had tabulated the responses to the questionnaire. In the six boxes I had drawn on the blackboard, they wrote the results of the survey:

	Marks
—Unable to converse with employers	885
—Lack of friends	782
—No opportunity to study	585
—Working conditions and employment	426
—Health and foods	328
—Living conditions and housing	210

It was not difficult for me to understand that their two priority problems revolved around communication and friendships. A strong barrier to integration in the Andean countries is not simply bi- or tri-lingualism, but rather the many and ususual idiomatic differences between regional tongues and their accompanying schisms in psycho-social habits. The conversations and dialogue that took place during these workshops resulted in such a mixture of Andean languages, idioms, semantic differences and linguistic idiosyncracies, that I have chosen to omit them for the purpose of this article.

A great discovery was made when the women realized that the most serious problem everyone had was the one that nobody talked about—the problem each had kept to herself: The fear of isolation, of being cut off from society. The sudden awareness of the group awakened these comments:

"Yes, it is true. This *is* our problem. We just don't understand each other. It's as if we were speaking different languages."[8]

"We can't—we don't know how to talk to our 'patrones'."

"We feel very alone and far away from the family."

"They never ask how we are getting along or if we have any problems."

"They expect us to cook and clean *their* way and do things we've never done before, but nobody shows us how. When we do it wrong, they get mad."

"We didn't have electricity in our village, so I was frightened when sparks came from the light cords."

"They command us, order us around, shriek at us if we do something wrong—but they never want to hear any explanation of our problems."

"The *'patrona'* wants me to bathe every day, but in my village everybody knows that will make you sick, so I am scared."

Gradually the verbalizing of these complaints began to be associated with parallel problems:

"The families and friends of almost everyone here are a long way from Lima, so there isn't any place we can go or anyone with whom we can share our problems—no one to give us advice."

"Since we can't read letters or write them, we are completely isolated and alone in the world."

By the ninth meeting, we had made great progress toward accomplishing one of the main objectives of the course: to enable each person to identify her own problems and place them in perspective according to her environment. Another objective, no less important, still remained: to look for and understand the reasons for these problems. I felt apprehensive because I knew that persuading people to look critically at themselves and analyze their attitudes objectively was always difficult. I began by cautiously suggesting, "Now that we've actually identified what our most important problems are, why don't we try to see what causes them? We know that the *'patrones'* don't understand us nor we, them. But why? Let's begin to look inside ourselves. Let's look at some of our own ideas and attitudes."

I did not expect them to respond immediately. In fact, I hoped only that in the eight weeks which had passed, I had been able to gain enough of their confidence and trust for them at least to reflect on my words.

"Someone said awhile ago that although she and her *'patrona'* both speak Spanish, it's as if they speak two separate languages. Could this be so? Do you think there's a possibility that if you were to polish up your Spanish—improve your grammar— maybe use words more carefully—your *'patrona'* would understand you better? Maybe if you were to learn to read and write, it'd be easier to keep in touch with others better," I suggested.

---

[8]Refers to communication between house-servants and employers. Very few had their own place to live; the majority lived in the employers' homes.

One girl, after thinking a minute, spoke up, "You're right, *'Senorita'* Jenny—since we can't read, we probably don't use lots of words correctly—at least, not the way they do in books or school. Maybe if we could learn to read, we could say better what we mean and then we wouldn't have to 'shut up' all the time."

I knew that my final task, yet to be accomplished, was getting the women to realize that only they could do something about their own situation. It would be easier if they would collaborate with and support each other's effort. In our final workshop, I suggested that we develop a "plan of action" to concentrate on this greatest problem.

"Besides learning to read and write, what else could we do to make more conversation and have better understanding between oursleves and our employers?" I asked.

One responded, hopefully, " *'Senorita,'* it would really be good if you would go to my employer's house and explain to her about our problems."

At once, at least 30 women chimed in unison, "Mine, too! Please talk to my *'patrona,'* too!"

Then a thoughtful voice spoke up, "Another idea has just occured to me. My *'patrona'* lies in bed all morning just reading magazines. Why don't you write something special about our problems for a magazine that many *'patronas'* would read? That would help us all."

"No, no," another girl interrupted, "it would be better to do it on the radio!"

Others now were getting excited. "No—it would be even better to do it on TV. All the rich have television!" Many agreed.

Someone else threw in another idea, "All our *'patronas'* go to Mass on Sundays. Why don't we ask the Rector to mention it when he talks about all those other things?"

I jumped to take advantage of this last suggestion, "I think this has lots of possibilities. Why don't a group of you form a committee to go and talk to the Rector? I'll help you if I can." Finally, I had found a way to get the women to take a first step toward group action. They had reached a milestone: they had identified a problem, analyzed some of its causes, and tried to find a solution. It was, perhaps, the critical step toward mending forty "broken wings."

Although the experiences I have shared here were motivated by my concern for poor rural women, I would like to point out that when we speak of "integrating" women who are on the margin of society, our responsibility is not only to the illiterate. I contend that a large percentage of educated women contribute nothing to improving society, neither as individuals nor as equal partners of the "human couple." They may feel superior, they may wear fine clothes and expensive jewelry, they may live in beautiful homes and be plump from rich foods; and yes, they may have maids like the *"patronas"* I have just written about. But if a person accepts what society has imposed on her, if she does not participate in making the decisions that affect her life and the lives of her children, if she allows others to make them for her—and if she makes no positive contribution other than bearing children (also about which she usually has little to say), then what is the difference between this woman and the *"campesina?"*

160

In some ways, the educated woman should be of even more concern to society since she has acquired the "tools" of communication, but often is unable or chooses not to use them to any advantage. Certainly, many do not use their education to accelerate the country's social and economic development. Whether one has the "tools" and the ability and does not use them—or has the ability but no opportunity to develop the "tools"—it is a waste either way. Both the educated and the illiterate suffer equally from psychological, social and moral malnutrition, and in their starvation, they sustain themselves on each other's weaknesses, to the denigration of both.

The integration of women into our social, political and economic structure will require two essential changes in the Peruvian value system. First, we will be obliged to destroy the barriers that separate the social classes. Secondly, women will have to become mutually supportive, regardless of social status, ideology, caste, profession and educational level. Such changes in our value system will come slowly, but as individuals we can each influence such changes through our children, our friends, our husbands, families and institutions. I am committed to adding my small contribution, and recognize the usefulness of self-analysis and self-evaluation as an aid in guiding rural women. It would work as well for urban dwellers, professional women, "patronas," students, and anyone who is willing to be honest with themselves, educated or uneducated. The important point is that the "broken wing" of our society cannot be mended until all of us, as integral parts of that wing, stop perpetuating and reinforcing the notion that women are incapable of serious thinking, not worth educating, and are only useful as breeding mares and draft animals, or lovely ornaments and toys to liven up life and enhance the status of the "other half."

SAVING MONEY WITH BIO-GAS

Ligia Cock Alvear (Colombia)

Ligia Cock Alvear became a graduate architect at the age of twenty-four, just in time to take over the philanthropic effort of her parents, Juan de Dios Cock Arango and Isabel Alvear de Cock. A devout Catholic and socially-conscious family, they were motivated by their belief that woman, as mother, plays an indispensible role in society as the family counselor and teacher, and that this applies to the poor as well as the rich. Ligia remembers that her father, an engineer, always said, "To have children is to obligate oneself to the task of raising human beings that are prepared and able to secure happiness for themselves and those they bring into the world." Thus, the Cock family philanthropic effort took the form of a day-care center for the children of poor working mothers. Ligia reflects the family philosophy in her concern for preparing mothers to confront the problems of raising children—with or without husbands—as well as for the children, themselves.

Although Ligia is from a family of ten children (five girls and five boys), when her father died in 1971, it was she who took over the responsibility of the center. She had been graduated from the Bolivarian Pontifical University in Medellin, with a degree in Urban Architecture; and had done post-graduate studies in architecture at the Catholic University of Louvain in Belgium, and the National University of Colombia in Bogota. Her preparation as an architect was providential in that she personally was able to design and supervise the construction of a new building to house the center, as well as taking over as chairman of its board of directors.

For the past ten years, Ligia has devoted over half her time, completely unremunerated, to the center's affairs. She spends many a night working into the wee hours to fulfill her architectural responsibilities so that she can continue to earn a living. Her professional assignments have included residences, schools, university and institutional housing, a home for the elderly, and several chapels in addition to the center. She is especially interested in low-cost housing problems. She is continually involved in research and in seeking solutions to living accommodations that can be placed within the reach of every family regardless of their income level. In 1968, this interest led her to study ways of producing low-cost energy, and to the design of a methane generator for the center. She has also patented a mechanical device designed to help people teach themselves to read, learn new languages, and other basic educational information.

In spite of the fact that Ligia is an attractive and very feminine woman, she has never married. At the time when she began her studies at the university, architecture was considered a "man's career." Of her class, which began with 45 men and two women, only nine men and Ligia were graduated. She has worked hard to gain professional respect in a traditionally male field. Her alert and creative mind is constantly exploring new avenues for taking advantage of readily available natural resources and low-cost materials. She is continually seeking efficient and inexpensive methods to disseminate information and knowledge to women in rural areas who have little access to education.

If you should ask Ligia, however, what is her greatest hope for the future, she will probably tell you, "...to assure a permanent flow of income for the center...there are so many courses for the women that we've had to cut back for lack of funds...the courses in veterinary training, small industries, human relations, first aid..."

At present, Ligia is associated with the architectural firm of Ramirez, Gutierrez and Co., in Medellin, and is an advisor to the National Service for Trade Apprentices (SENA) for the construction of bio-gas generators in the rural areas of Colombia.

SAVING MONEY WITH BIO-GAS

by

Ligia Cock Alvear

We recently submitted to a European philanthropic organization a proposal for fnancial assistance to help us in expanding the bio-gas system which provides low-cost fuel for our center "Jesus Amigo de la Infancia (JIF)."[1] The Center, a non-profit corporation established 20 years ago for the children of poor working mothers, has had to struggle all its life to stay alive. Because of its economy, the bio-gas system, in operation for 10 of these years, has been a critical factor in the Center's survival. With the rising costs of energy, its expansion is now of fundamental importance. The European organization, after some months of consideration, politely informed us that the request had been refused. Their decision, they said, was based on the fact that they felt it was extremely doubtful that the bio-gas system, as it was designed, could work.

I wanted to shout, "But it's BEEN working fine for 10 years! Can't you read?" I had carefully outlined, I thought, the history of the Center "Jesus Amigo," how and why we had developed the bio-gas system, its proven benefits, and the advantages of expanding it. It appeared that either they had not read the proposal carefully, or they simply did not *believe* that the system was in operation.

Experiences like this are all the more frustrating because organizations like JIF must depend on public and private financial support. There are many sources of such support, particularly in the industrially-developed countries, that have been created especially to provide financial assistance for Third World "development." Yet, it seems that many of us who make the greatest personal sacrifices, have the most difficult time convincing such wealthy *"patrones"* that our efforts are worthy of their support. We are again in the *"peon-patron"* relationship of having to beg for handouts for economic survival, while trying to maintain our human dignity for social survival. The doubt cast on the operability of the bio-gas system was like saying, "How could such a technical innovation be successfully designed by a woman, let alone one who is running a nursery school for the poor in a developing country?"

The reader may well be thinking that there are other criteria to be considered when deciding how best to allocate money for development programs intended to improve the lives of the poor. One must look at the competence and reliability of the requesting organization, its objectives and overall goal, and certainly its credibility and acceptance by the people it is trying to help. One must always ask if the leaders are capable of doing what they say they will do, and finally—a favorite question—"Can the organization become self-sufficient?" I always find myself answering, silently of course, "We could be self-sufficient if we took in children of wealthy parents instead of poor," or "Perhaps we could package human waste and sell it on the street corner."

It is true that my design and development of the bio-gas system did not begin with my knowledge of science, nor with the intention of obtaining a patent and going

---

[1]Jesus, the Children's Friend Center

into mass production to earn money. It was not the *raison d'etre*, nor conceived as even a part of the dream that motivated the creation of the Center. Rather, it was developed as a response to our continual problems of poverty, in the hope that it might be one answer—hopefully, a permanent one—to the ever-increasing costs of keeping the Center alive. Please keep in mind that we serve three meals a day to 22 children who sleep at the Center during the week and 8 who go home after dinner in the evenings, as well as the staff. Moreover, we give short courses for the mothers in nursing, cooking, small crafts and sewing; and one-day seminars on topics such as education of children, adolescence and responsible parenthood. But, let me take you back to the beginning...

The Center "Jesus Amigo de la Infancia," as with most things in Colombia, could not have been conceived in its entirety at the beginning. Not only was there not enough money to plan very far ahead—it simply would never have gotten started if we had had to wait until there was enough. It began with a dream in 1959, and then grew as its needs increasingly imposed their demands.

The dream started in the *Barrio Campo Valdes*, a poor neighborhood of Medellin, where my idealistic parents thought they could do something to change the lives of the underprivileged children who spilled into its streets and crowded its alleys. A great percentage of the mothers in this neighborhood are unmarried, and do their best to earn a living usually working as domestic servants. The average income of these women is between 600 to 1,300 Colombian pesos a month.[2]

Many of these unwed mothers are totally alone in the world and unable to pay rent for even a small corner of a room in which to live. They cannot provide food for their little ones without begging or stealing. It is not unusual for women like this to tie up their children while they are away for fear they will wander off and be lost or killed. One often hears about children who die of suffocation, are burned in fires, scalded by boiling water, or bitten by rabid animals—these are the ones left alone. Then there are the women who scrape together a few pesos to pay an acquaintance to feed and look after the babies, discovering when it is too late that the child spends its days hungry and uncared for because the money was used for something else. It is not difficult to imagine the moral problems, the psychological trauma, and even physical deformities that occur as a result of leaving children unattended, and the damaging effects of these experiences on our future citizens.

The original idea that motivated my parents was to provide a day-care center for the children of the most desperate of these mothers so that the women could be free to work and earn a living without worrying constantly about their children and thus, defeating the purpose. Secondly, they wanted to ensure that the youngest and most vulnerable of these little ones be spared the frightening experiences that often render their adult lives useless. Lastly, they wanted to educate the women, themselves, to broaden their understanding of their reality, and to enrich their lives.

The Center began in the improvised shelter of a decaying house, but it was better than nothing. We had only the basic necessities and our difficulties were innumerable, not the least of which were demands by the government that we do

---

[2]About U.S. $15.00-$45.00/month.

something about the exterior appearance of the building. Their threats to close us down united the parents in waging a war of petitions and memorandums in protest which at least, had the effect of silencing the officials who had nothing in the way of solutions or assistance to offer.

Money has always been our greatest problem. The Corporation takes the responsibility and shoulders the principal burden of the operating expenses. The parents contribute what they can, according to their financial ability. Of course, there are some who cannot afford to pay at all. We live from month to month, often on the meagre proceeds from raffles, food sales, and other donations we beg to augment the funds which frequently sink to zero. The effort we put forth to obtain the greatest possible return from our resources is enormous. Economizing has become a way of life—in the food we serve the children, striving to provide sufficient quantity without loss of nutrition; in the pre-school materials for teaching; in every activity we develop—and we are staffed by volunteers.

The Center struggled along for nine years, until a member of a religious order, retired from her community of nuns, decided to devote her time to raising the money to build a decent building. I was on the Board of Directors and offered to contribute my services without compensation, to design and supervise the construction of the new day school and child care center. We pinched each penny to squeeze the very most from it. Materials of good quality were used, but we allowed no luxury items, no unused spaces, and nothing that was not functional. Incorporated into the plans were only those things that were absolutely essential for the activities to be carried out in the building, and to insure a pleasant and clean environment. Where possible, we eliminated whitewash and plaster, taking advantage of this opportunity to expose the building structure to educate the children to learn to reject the false and unnecessary. Given our financial constraints, I particularly looked for a way to provide a continuing source of low-cost energy for the facility. After much research, I designed and built a bio-gas generator which converts the organic wastes from the bathrooms and scraps from the kitchen, into energy. For ten years, this system has supplied most of the cooking fuel for the Center.

169

The bio-gas system, therefore, plays an important role in the economic viability of the Center. Without it, it is doubtful that the Center could continue serving three hot meals a day. This may not be seen as complete independence, but it is as close to self-sufficiency as we can come at this time. I believe it may be meaningful to other organizations like ourselves, who must make every penny count.

In developing countries like Colombia, particularly in the rural areas, toilets that flush and modern plumbing are considered luxuries few can afford. The bio-gas system which requires a minimum of eight persons to produce waste on a daily basis, is ideal for institutions in rural areas such as small schools and clinics, but it requires a special drainage system to take maximum advantage of the organic wastes produced.

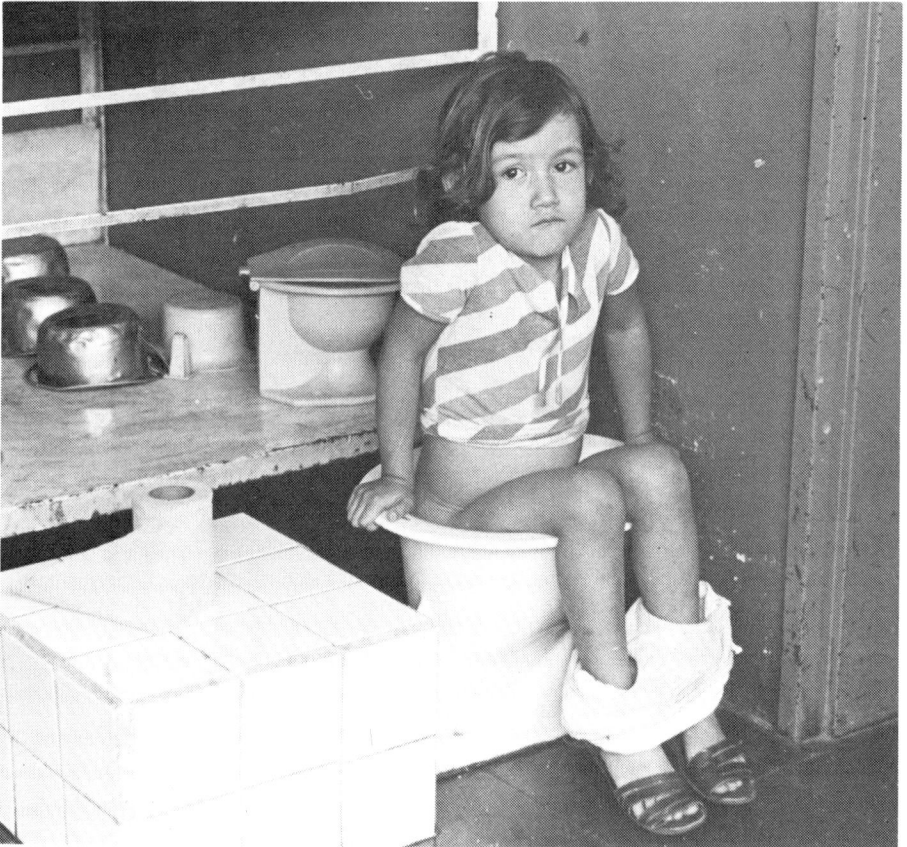

Modern bathroom plumbing systems are based on the use of large volumes of water each time a toilet is flushed, while kitchen and laundry drains carry great quantities of detergents. Both detergents and water in large amounts interfere with the production of methane gas, the final product we are seeking. The bio-gas system is especially useful in areas where water is scarce or has to be hand-carried, and where expensive modern plumbing is not only inappropriate, but unheard of.

I began by designing a network of conduits from the bathrooms and kitchen to a centrally-located holding tank on the ground floor. The function of these conduits is to separate the useable wastes from the drainage water that normally is used to wash them into the sewer or septic tanks. Toilet paper is of little significance; as long as it does not contain plastic substances, it will decompose along with the human wastes. We were able to control the amount of water in the system by using "country toilets" in the children's lavatories. The "country toilet" has a vitreous bowl which is smaller than the usual toilet, and has no water tank for flushing. The children are taught to flush them with water from a little bucket that is easily filled from a nearby faucet. Cleanliness is accomplished with a much smaller volume of

water than that used by the ordinary toilet. In addition, these little "country toilets" are inexpensive, have no plumbing mechanisms that need maintenance or replacement of parts, are never out-of-order, use a minimum of water, and their size is ideal for children.

We adapted the adult toilets to the system by placing large objects in the water tanks to displace the normal volume of water. This had the effect of reducing the amount of water used in the flushing process, without affecting the proper functioning of the apparatus.

The generator and storage tanks were located in a patio adjacent to the kitchen and the laundry. This was a central point halfway between the bathrooms and the utility areas, yet close to the actual cooking area where the gas would be burned. The generator, as you can see from the drawing included here, comprises six main elements:

1. **The anaerobic digestion tank.** In order to facilitate the process of converting the waste matter or bio-mass into gas, this tank must be completely air-tight. The digestion of the bacteria which takes place inside is exactly the opposite of that which occurs in septic tanks.

2. **The chamber or chambers to hold the organic wastes prior to their introduction to the anaerobic digestion tank.** Our system uses three: one for kitchen scraps; and two for toilet wastes.

3. **An apparatus in which to store the gas.** Our design uses a mobile fiber-glass bell that has a siphon at the top with a mechanism that can be squeezed and clamped to control the passage of air.

4. **A bushing** (in the uppermost part of the bell) for the conduit that channels the gas to the combustion chamber.

5. **The connecting tubes** that run from the organic waste-holding chambers to the anaerobic digestion tank. These tubes are located at the base of the holding chambers and function by the force of gravity.

6. **The overflow.** A canal that provides an escape to the municipal sewage system for excess wastes in the event more are produced than can be stored for introduction to the digestion tank.

It is important to point out that the period for retaining the bio-mass in the digestion tank should be of sufficient duration to assure *complete* digestion, for it is only in this way that the production of gas can be achieved with genuine effectiveness and economy. In addition, it is imperative that the quantity of water in the system be kept to a minimum; otherwise, the liquid will be discharged from the chamber too rapidly, and as a result, gas lost. The operating temperature is also of critical importance. To function most effectively, it should be maintained between 27 °C and 37 °C. The most economical way of maintaining this level is through solar energy.

Eventually, I plan to expand our production of bio-gas by adding solar power to our current generator. This, of course, was the basis of our request to the European

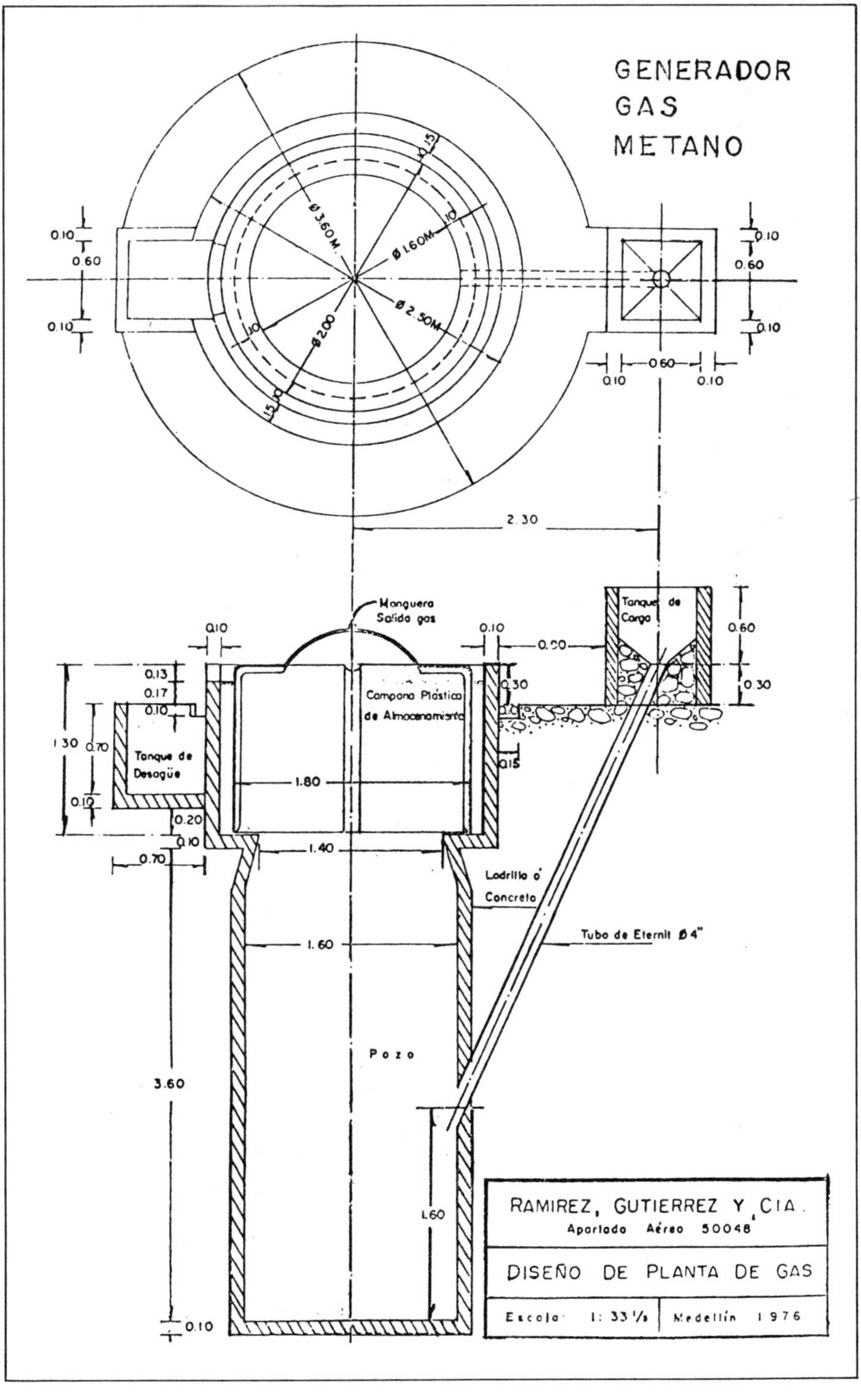

GENERADOR
GAS
METANO

0.10
0.60
Ø 3.60 M
Ø 1.60M–10
Ø 2.00
Ø 2.50 M.
0.10
0.60
0.10
0.60
0.10
0.60
0.10

2.30

Manguera
Salida gas

Tanque de
Carga
0.60
0.30

0.10
0.60
0.30
0.15

0.13
0.17
0.10

Campana Plástica
de Almacenamiento

1.30
0.70
Tanque de
Desagüe
0.10
0.20
0.10
0.70

1.80
1.40

Ladrillo o
Concreto

Tubo de Eternit Ø 4"

1.60

3.60

Pozo

1.60

0.10

RAMIREZ, GUTIERREZ Y CIA.
Apartado Aéreo 50048

DISEÑO DE PLANTA DE GAS

Escala: 1: 33 ⅓ | Medellín 1976

173

philanthropic organization.

Bio-gas generators like the one I have designed, produce methane gas that has sufficient caloric power to cook food in a third of the time taken by an electric stove. The Center cooks daily in an hour and a half, the same amount of food that would require four hours of electricity. Were we to add a solar heater to our present generator, we could greatly increase the amount of time that the gas would last. In other words, the gas would burn longer while retaining the same caloric power. This would make it possible to heat our water with bio-gas, in addition to cooking the food.

One of the beauties of the bio-gas technology is the final waste product which is almost as clear as potable water and notable for its almost total absence of odor. Because of its organic substance, it makes a superior fertilizer which has great advantages over commercial chemical products. The Center produces more organic waste than our present system can utilize; consequently, we have connected the overflow canal out of the tank to the sewer pipe in the street. It breaks my heart that we are able to utilize only a small part of its potential, since exploiting it fully would require an initial investment that we cannot afford to make at this time.

Nevertheless, JIF has found many ways to provide extra services without increasing operating costs. We have access to final year medical students (interns) and their professors at the Children's Hospital of Medellin, which offers medical care for our children and staff, free of charge. In addition, in 1979, for the first time, we were granted assistance from the Department of Education in the form of a grant equivalent to approximately U.S. $750.00, as well as two teachers whose salaries are paid by the government to work at the Center. To some this will sound like a mere "drop in the bucket," but without it JIF would not have been able to open its doors this year.

My everlasting concern is to find a sufficiently stable economic answer that will keep the Center running, and enable us to go beyond our present approach with the mothers of Barrio Campo Valdes.

No one is more aware than I that energy and fuel is only one small part of our concerns, albeit an important one. When the founder of the Center died in 1971, the year the new building was completed, I was elected president of the Corporation with all the responsibility that implies. In the beginning, I felt innundated by the plethora of problems that had to be dealt with, seemingly at once. I've learned that the Center is like a living body: to be healthy, all the organic parts have to be in good condition and function simultaneously. I also recognize that caring for the children of poor working mothers is not the only, nor perhaps even the best solution to their problems. But it is the first step in searching for a better solution—a temporary "band-aid" which, while not eradicating the cause, at least helps to avoid the more immediate and extreme remedies that might be sought in desperate cases. After all, you don't want the patient to bleed to death while you look for the person who shot him. Caring for the children provides the opportunity and allows the time necessary to seek alternative answers and ways to eradicate the social diseases that form the root of the problems. And in the process, we gain the trust of the community, an absolutely essential element if the Center is to make any valuable inroads. Meanwhile, we have to keep from going broke.

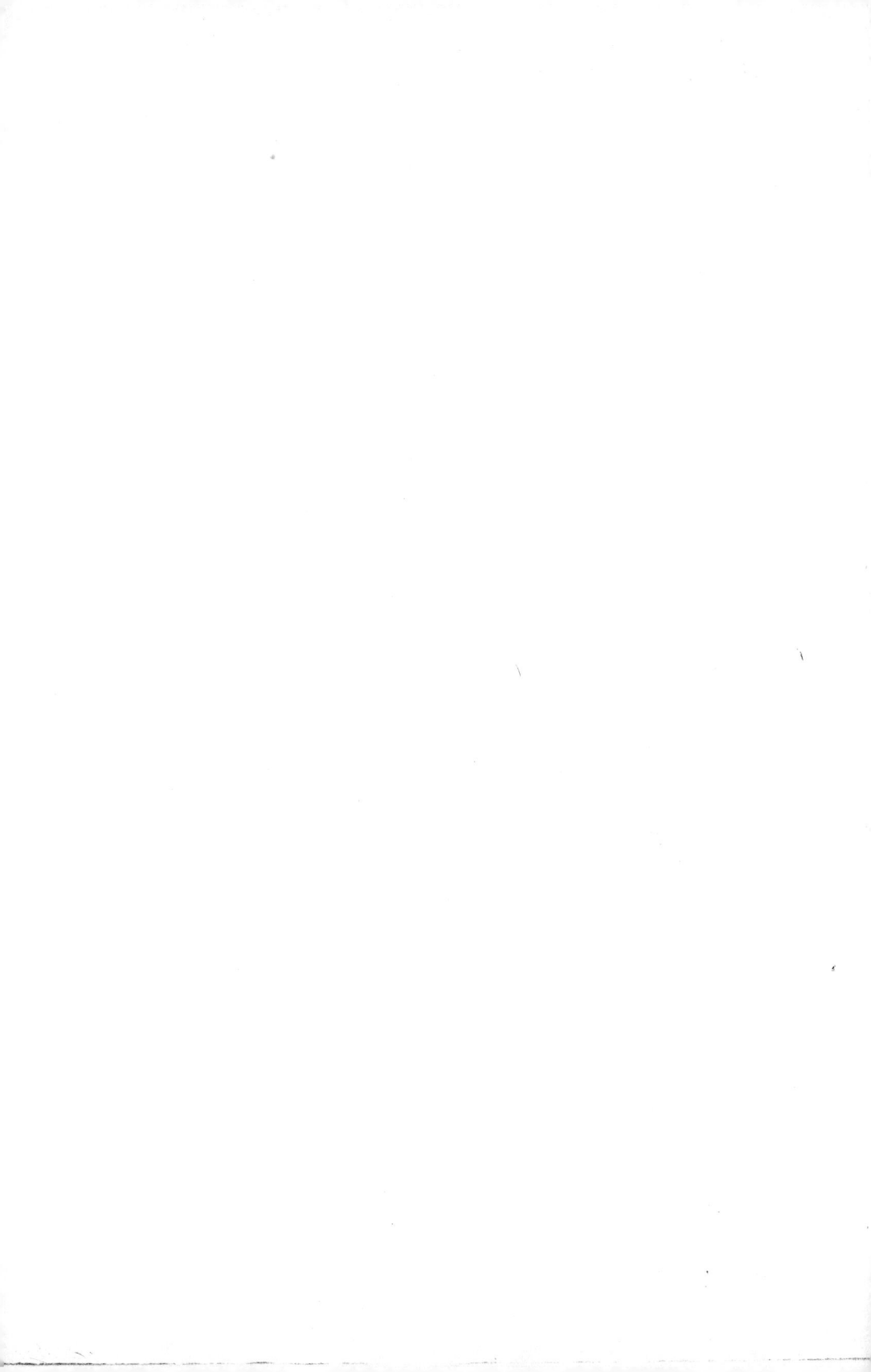